'This book presents a salient truth: every investor – no matter how large or small – has the power to help address our climate crisis and build a more sustainable world. Together, we can and must act now'
Al Gore, former Vice President of the United States

'I can't imagine a more important book at the moment. A detailed, action-orientated guide on how to make our money matter and save us and the planet we live on'
Richard Curtis, writer, director, Co-founder of Red Nose Day and UN Sustainable Development Goals Advocate

'Investing responsibly is one of the most powerful avenues towards addressing climate change. But it's not only for large institutional investors. Every person's savings account and pension can meaningfully contribute. Ross tells us how in this clear, easy-to-understand yet transformative book'
Christiana Figueres, Founding Partner, Global Optimism and former Executive Secretary, United Nations Framework Convention on Climate Change

'People often ask me what THEY can do to act on the climate crisis. I now have yet another answer. *Investing to Save the Planet* explains the power you have, through your financial investment choices, to accelerate the path towards a sustainable clean-energy future. Read this book and be empowered to create a better future for the planet'
Michael Mann, Distinguished Professor, Penn State University, author of *The New Climate War*

'Changing the way that we invest is one of the most powerful levers we have for solving climate change. This hugely interesting and immensely practical book not only explains why changing how we invest is so critically important but also provides a set of powerful tools for actually doing it'
Rebecca Henderson, John and Natty McArthur University Professor at Harvard University and author of *Reimagining Capitalism*

ABOUT THE AUTHOR

Alice Ross has been a *Financial Times* journalist for more than a decade, writing on topics from personal investment to corporate activity to market movements. She has held roles as deputy editor of the weekend 'Money' section, Editor of the *Wealth* magazine and Editor of the *FT* newsletter, 'Trade Secrets', which examines issues affecting globalisation including climate change. Alice has a degree in philosophy from Cambridge University and an MA in European Thought from University College London.

Investing to Save the Planet

ALICE ROSS

BUSINESS

PENGUIN BUSINESS

UK | USA | Canada | Ireland | Australia
India | New Zealand | South Africa

Penguin Business is part of the Penguin Random House group of companies
whose addresses can be found at global.penguinrandomhouse.com.

First published 2020
001

Set in 13.5/16 pt Garamond MT Std
Text design by Couper Street Type Co.
Typeset by Jouve (UK), Milton Keynes
Printed and bound in Great Britain by Clays Ltd, Elcograf S.p.A.

A CIP catalogue record for this book is available from the British Library

ISBN: 978–0–241–45723–8

Follow us on LinkedIn: https://www.linkedin.com/company/penguin-connect

www.greenpenguin.co.uk

Penguin Random House is committed to a
sustainable future for our business, our readers
and our planet. This book is made from Forest
Stewardship Council® certified paper.

To Greta and Ranald

Contents

Preface

I had the idea to write this book, which started life as an article for the *Financial Times*, in the summer of 2019. Climate change was in the news, and it wasn't pretty. The Amazon was burning – literally. July was the hottest month on record. Every day I seemed to be waking up to some new climate crisis, and I felt powerless to do anything about it. At the time, I was the wealth editor at the *Financial Times*. I spent a lot of my time talking to rich people and private bankers. That was where I first heard about some of the climate change solutions that people were investing in: new technologies that could change the world, and that needed deep pockets to finance them. But then I thought: surely the average investor on the street could get involved too, by looking at what was in their pension fund, for example, or thinking about whether they should invest in fossil fuel companies. It seemed to me that explaining what we can do to fight climate change as investors as well as consumers would give people some sense of control over the situation.

Looking back at that time, some things have changed. The bad news we got used to waking up to in 2020 was of course the coronavirus: the daily death tolls, the hit to the economy. The climate crisis seemed almost to have been sidelined. I wrote much of this book in lockdown at my home in London while my two young children were out of school. It was a busy, stressful time.

But it was also a quiet time. I was woken up, like so many others, not by planes roaring overhead to Heathrow but by birdsong. Pollution was on track to fall by a record level. Neighbours started swapping food and shopping for each other. We stood in the street and clapped for our health workers every Thursday evening. It felt like a connected time.

And people started to notice how companies were handling the crisis. Some were firing their workers. Others were guaranteeing jobs. The investors in those companies started to notice too, and began speaking out. Our global collective experience of the coronavirus drew comparisons with climate change: both were a common enemy that would best be fought through cooperation. The experience of individuals and communities helping each other, and of investors caring whether the companies they owned were treating their workers well, gave people hope that much-needed cooperation on climate change would work too. 'Build Back Better' became a catchphrase as governments tried to figure out how to emerge from the economic crisis in the right way.

Anyone with savings, a pension or investments has building blocks at their disposal too. If we invest our money in the right way, we can help to combat climate change and feel a sense of control in an uncertain world. This book will help you to do that.

I

A Short History of Green Investing

When David Blood told his colleagues in 2003 that he was resigning to start a sustainable investment company, they laughed at him. Blood was a senior banker, working as the head of asset management at Goldman Sachs. His clients were among the largest investors in the world. But back then, not many of them were interested in investing in climate change solutions.* Most experts at that time, Blood recalls, thought that sustainable investing meant limiting your horizons. In other words, it was about being a do-gooder rather than an investor: people could choose not to invest in fossil fuel companies, but they'd make less money as a result. 'We believed differently,' he says.

---

* Goldman Sachs would later achieve notoriety in the wake of the global financial crisis of 2008 after a scathing article in *Rolling Stone* magazine likened it to a great 'vampire squid' whose aim was to create 'pure profit for rich individuals'.

Blood joined forces with Al Gore, the former vice president of the United States, who in 2000 had narrowly lost the presidency to George W. Bush. Gore was fast becoming a leading figure in the climate change debate. In 2006, he released a critically acclaimed and widely watched documentary, *An Inconvenient Truth*, which warned about the dangers of climate change. The following year, he won the Nobel Peace Prize for helping to raise awareness of global warming.* The rest of the world – consumers and, importantly, investors – was waking up to climate change, both to the risks it posed, and then to the opportunities. Now, Gore sees investment as key to unlocking some of the problems of cutting carbon emissions. 'We believe that the world is in the early stages of a sustainability revolution,' he says.

The company that Blood and Gore founded, Generation Investment Management, is now one of the most successful investors in climate change solutions. In fact, it is one of the most successful investment managers full stop. Its flagship global equity fund returned more than 11 per cent a year on average to investors between its launch in 2005 and March 2020, compared to an average 6 per cent a year from its benchmark, the MSCI World Index. And it has been followed by countless other sustainable investment specialists. Investing with the

---

* Gore was a joint winner with the Intergovernmental Panel on Climate Change (IPCC). The prize was awarded for their efforts to 'build up and disseminate greater knowledge about man-made climate change, and to lay the foundations for the measures that are needed to counteract such change'.

environment in mind has become extremely popular, with investment houses falling over themselves to market new products to consumers – or, as they are known, retail investors.

What has changed between the turn of the century and now? Until very recently, sustainable investment was seen as a specialist, niche area. It was assumed that investing responsibly meant that you wouldn't make as much money. Investing ethically was more of a hobby, or a philanthropic pursuit. A serious investor who wanted to make real money shouldn't be troubled too much by morals, went the thinking. Things could hardly be more different now.

Ethical investing in its modern form can be traced back decades: from investors shunning companies profiting from South African apartheid in the 1970s and 80s to those dumping tobacco holdings in the 90s. Investing with the environment in mind started as a niche area in broader ethical investment, but it shared a key characteristic: it was about avoiding things – in this case, fossil fuel companies. As it became obvious that the world needed more renewable energy, investors started to see positive opportunities too. The first years of this century saw venture capitalists and private equity funds pour millions into solar and wind energy technologies.

This proved to be an early setback for the environmental investment movement, however. First, government subsidies made it hard to value the market properly and oversupply led prices to fall. And then came the global financial crisis of 2008. The collapse in financial markets heaped pressure on a sector that had already been struggling. Lots of renewable energy companies went bust, and investors lost millions. Big oil majors like BP and Shell who had tentatively dipped a toe in the water of solar energy rapidly pulled out, believing it to be unprofitable. Some people reverted to their view that investing sustainably was a mug's game.

Since then, however, there have been major changes in the way mainstream investors think about the environment, and crucially in how they think about risk. From government pension funds to billion-dollar investment funds to hedge fund tycoons, everyone in finance is waking up to the fact that climate change is going to change the world, so we had better change our investment portfolios as well. The recent explosion in interest in sustainable investment can be traced back to two key moments in recent history: the 2015 Paris Agreement, and the publication of the UN sustainable development goals the same year.

In September 2015, the United Nations published 17 sustainable development goals as part of its 2030 Agenda for Sustainable Development. All UN members signed up to implement the goals, which range from no poverty and zero hunger to climate action and responsible consumption and production, and are intended to be achieved by 2030.

Later that year, representatives from all corners of the globe met at the UN climate change conference in Paris to discuss ways to combat the growing climate crisis.

Nearly every country in the world agreed to limit the increase in the global average temperature to well below 2 degrees Centigrade above pre-industrial levels, with an aim of limiting the increase to just 1.5 degrees. The 2 degrees target would require carbon dioxide emissions to peak by 2020 then be reduced to 'net zero' before the end of the century. Net zero doesn't mean that there wouldn't be any carbon dioxide emissions, but that any remaining emissions would be offset through other measures, from planting trees on the low-tech end to carbon capture and storage on the high-tech end. To limit warming to 1.5 degrees, net zero needs to happen by 2050. Various countries and companies have set themselves net zero targets by 2050 as a result, including the United Kingdom, Norway and New Zealand, and oil companies BP and Shell.

The year the world woke up to climate change

Developments since 2015 have hastened the interest in climate change solutions, as global warming has led to volatile weather conditions, economic damage and increasing species extinction. According to analysts at UBS, 2019 was the year the world really woke up to climate change, following a report from the UN Intergovernmental Panel on Climate Change (IPCC) the previous year, which set out a stark difference in outcomes for people around the world even in the event of a 2 degrees change versus a 1.5 degrees change. This growing sense that climate change, far from being a niche concern, was the most important problem the world faced thrust it into the mainstream. Politicians and celebrities alike burnished their green credentials. New poster children for the movement emerged – literally, in the case of Greta Thunberg, the Swedish environmental activist who shot to fame at the age of just 15, having pioneered the movement for school students to strike over the climate in 2018, and who told attendees of the 2019 Davos summit that 'our house is on fire'.

Waking up to climate change in the investment world means looking to see where risks can be avoided and profits can be made. A report by Bank of America declared that the 2020s 'are shaping up to be the decade of climate opportunity', predicting that what it calls the climate solutions market could double in value from $1tn to $2tn by 2025.

The general public has taken note. More and more people want their investments to be sustainable and are conscious of where their money is going. A report by the UK's Department for International Development found that 68 per cent of UK savers wanted their investments to consider the impact on people and planet alongside financial performance. Record sums of money were poured into sustainable investment funds in 2019 by US investors alone, with nearly four times as much – $20.6bn – ploughed into US sustainable investment funds as in the previous year, according to Morningstar, the data provider. Appetite was even stronger in Europe, where European investors pumped more than twice as much cash into sustainable funds in 2019 as in the previous year, totalling a record €120bn.

Ethical investing used to be about avoiding things. But green or sustainable investing is now about finding opportunities as well. The investment world is on the cusp of a huge transformation in the way it thinks about risks and making money. Because this change in mind-set is taking place right now, though, the sands are still shifting on a lot of important things, such as what sustainable investing really is, or should be, how regulators should define it and how investors should do it.

When retail investors – that's you and me, as opposed to institutional investors, who run things like pension funds – say they want to invest to save the planet, they usually mean one of two things: they want to avoid certain companies, usually oil and gas companies; or they want to invest in companies, usually smaller, newer ones, that are explicitly helping to reduce carbon emissions. These could be wind farm companies like Vestas, alternative meat companies like Beyond Meat, or green transport companies like Tesla. But when institutional investors offer you a sustainable fund, they might mean something quite different. They could just be investing in 'best in class' companies in their sector, for example, so you might find yourself owning companies that seem to have nothing to do with the environment, like Starbucks or Microsoft. Or they could be investing in companies in transition, so you might find yourself still owning oil and gas companies. As we'll see later in the book, this misalignment between institutional and retail investors in terms of their understanding of sustainable investing can sometimes be a problem.

The alphabet soup

The fund management industry does not help itself with its alphabet soup of terminology. The terms 'sustainable investing', 'ethical investment' and 'socially responsible investing' (SRI) are often used interchangeably and usually refer to investments that are made not just with financial returns in mind, but take account of an investor's values and morals as well. SRI is the older term, and people who have already dipped a toe in the water of sustainable investing will probably recognise it. In the past, it didn't necessarily have anything to do with climate change – if you didn't want to hold tobacco stocks, for example, that would class you as an ethical, or socially responsible, investor.

These days, the main term used by the financial industry for all socially responsible investment is ESG (environmental, social and governance). ESG investing is intended to be more financially rigorous: investors are supposed to be considering the way in which ESG risks and opportunities can affect companies' financial returns. Sustainable funds tend to have this ESG acronym somewhere in their name. In theory, an investor could select companies with high ESG ratings purely because they believe their performance is likely to be better, rather than for any ethical reason.

On a global level, the percentage of both retail and institutional investors applying ESG principles to at least a quarter of their portfolios jumped from 48 per cent in 2017 to 75 per cent in 2019, according to a report from Deloitte. This enthusiasm is only expected to grow. In February 2020, Deloitte predicted that ESG funds could make up 50 per cent of the total of professionally managed investments by 2025. But do all these ESG investors know that they're not necessarily investing to help the environment?

People who want to invest to save the planet should do their homework before picking an ESG fund, as it might invest in companies that score highly only on the social or governance side. A company might be in an ESG fund if it has a good environmental score – a renewable energy company, for example. It might be ESG if it has a good social score – it treats its workers well. And it might be ESG if it has a good governance score – it has fair bonus schemes and holds its executives to account for their actions. So just because you invest in an ESG fund doesn't mean you're investing to save the planet. While climate change solutions funds are almost certainly going to be ESG funds, not all ESG funds include companies that care about the environment. It surprises a lot of investors to learn, for example, that oil giant BP is in some ESG funds because it scores well on governance. A report by UK wealth manager SCM Direct in 2019 found that the L&G Future World ESG UK Index, for example, had nearly 11 per cent of its holdings in tobacco, alcohol, gaming and defence stocks.

But even investing in the E of ESG is not always straightforward. Some companies may be in environmental funds because they are making something that will help to change the world – like alternative meat or hydrogen fuel cells. But others may be in such funds because, for example, the fund manager is pursuing a strategy of 'best in class'. It could be a fossil fuel company, but one that is investing more in renewable energy than its peers. It could be a global car company that is investing more in electric vehicles than its rivals. How you feel about this is your personal choice, but it may not be clear in the fund labelling.

With so many investment companies keen to jump on the ESG bandwagon and profit from the trend, there have been concerns about greenwashing. A play on the term whitewashing, where problems are covered up, greenwashing happens when companies or fund managers pretend their products are more environmentally friendly than they really are. Some financial advisers and investors worry that investment firms are launching new products to try and ride the recent wave of interest without putting too much thought into them. The fact that ESG labelling is currently so confusing for investors only makes it easier to greenwash.

Many fund managers have been quick to piggyback on the Paris Agreement when marketing environmental funds to consumers with a growing interest in climate change solutions. When the UN launched its 17 sustainable development goals (SDGs) in 2015, for example, it laid them out as a series of little coloured boxes with a logo on each one. Not all were directly climate change related – no poverty, zero hunger, and quality education were among the goals, for example. Others included climate action, affordable and clean energy, and clean water and sanitation. Fund managers now often say that their fund is investing in line with one or more of these goals. The well-designed logos have proven particularly impactful in marketing materials. 'The person who invented those icons should be given a job at [advertising giant] Saatchi, as every investment manager is using them,' jokes Michael Lewis, head of ESG thematic research at DWS, the German asset manager.

But some investors think fund houses are using these goals to try to make existing or new funds appear more relevant. Some funds have been renamed in recent years: Morningstar found that in 2019, more than 250 funds had repurposed themselves from traditional to sustainable. When it investigated, it found that in some cases fund managers had adapted a fund purely for marketing purposes, without changing the structure or investment philosophy. That doesn't mean the fund didn't change its holdings at all, but in some cases managers simply made tweaks, removing controversial companies. In October 2019, for example, the BMO European Equity fund was renamed the BMO Sustainable Opportunities European Equity. It made 'few changes', according to Morningstar, though it did remove Richemont, which owns British gunmaker James Purdey and Sons, as well as jewellery company Cartier, which was criticised by Human Rights Watch in 2018, among others, for failing to ensure that its jewels were ethically mined. Many fund managers tweak existing funds for regulatory reasons: new rules in Europe require fund managers to offer a sustainable product to investors who want one. But there is also a view in the investment industry that some managers create products that might be compared to spaghetti – throwing them at the wall to see what sticks – in order to take advantage of a trend.

One fund manager gives the example of water funds that say they invest in line with the SDG goal of clean water and sanitation. The goal is to address the lack of sanitation and improve access to safe drinking water, mainly in poor countries. Yet many water funds are stocked with Western utility companies, which, the manager says, 'are processing rich people's sewage when the problem is a lack of drinking water in the Third World. That dislocation and hypocrisy is important to avoid.'

A 2019 report from market researcher Cicero found that 97 out of 100 financial advisers were either very or fairly concerned about the possible mis-selling of products marketed as having strong ESG credentials as consumer interest in the responsible investment sector surged. Neville White, head of sustainable research at EdenTree, the asset manager that sponsored the research, told the *Financial Times* at the time that 'The language in this part of the market has become dense and confusing. There is little regulation over what you label a product.'

We'll look more at this issue of greenwashing in the course of the book.

'You know it must be serious'

Regardless of whether they're institutional or retail, investors around the world are starting to realise that they need to take climate change risk into account when considering whether to invest in a particular company or sector. There are various movements among professional investors to achieve this, which we'll look at later. Thousands of pension funds, foundations and institutional investors, for example, have signed up to the UN Principles for Responsible Investment (PRI), which require signatories to publicly report on their responsible investment activity.

Many professional investors are becoming increasingly outspoken on climate change – and, in a sign of how mainstream the issue has become, they are not necessarily running climate change funds or specialising in sustainable investment. Take Christopher Hohn, one of the world's best-known hedge fund managers. In an unusual crossover between the financial world and that of the eco-warrior, he backed the climate change movement Extinction Rebellion, which rose to prominence in 2019 after its supporters held sit-ins at key sites across London, blocking off major bridges and shutting down traffic. Hohn gave the movement £50,000 of his own money, making him its biggest individual donor, and contributed even more through his philanthropic fund. In December 2019, he said his activist hedge fund, TCI – which is not a sustainable investment specialist – would vote against directors at companies that failed to disclose their carbon dioxide emissions. As the *Financial Times* drily put it: 'When a hedge fund manager worries about the rest of humanity, you know it must be serious.'

The biggest investment manager in the world, Black-Rock, caused headlines in January 2020 when its chief executive, Larry Fink, wrote to the heads of the companies BlackRock invested in saying that there was about to be a 'significant reallocation of capital' as investors around the world considered how they should invest wisely given climate change. 'Every government, company, and shareholder must confront climate change,' he wrote – adding that BlackRock would be increasingly likely to vote against companies on sustainability grounds.

Whether promises by professional investors to consider climate change seriously can be taken at face value is something we will explore in this book. It is notable, for example, that Hohn has been one of BlackRock's most vocal critics, accusing the fund manager before its January letter of being 'full of greenwash'.

The muddy waters of 'green' billionaires

Finding solutions to climate change has proven to be a far cry from the philanthropic activity it was once believed to be. In fact it has made, and continues to make, some individuals extremely wealthy. Just as the Industrial Revolution of the nineteenth century created family dynasties like the Rockefellers and the Vanderbilts, today a new wave of entrepreneurs is accumulating wealth that is likely to last for generations. In January 2020, Bloomberg published a list of 'green billionaires' and predicted that there would be many more to follow in the next decade.

The most recognisable person on the list is Elon Musk, the founder of electric car company Tesla. But many of the new wave of green billionaires are not – or not yet – household names. Topping the list, one place ahead of Musk, are four shareholders in Chinese electric battery maker CATL, which supplies firms including Toyota and BMW: Zeng Yuqun, Huang Shilin, Pei Zhenhua, and Li Ping, who between them have a combined wealth of $16.7bn. Germany's Aloys Wobben, founder of Enercon, one of the world's largest wind turbine companies, made the list, as did Australia's Anthony Pratt of Pratt Industries, the world's largest privately held 100 per cent recycled paper and packaging company. Also on the list is Trevor Milton, founder of US start-up Nikola Motor, which develops hydrogen-powered trucks; and Spain's José Manuel Entrecanales, whose Acciona company is a huge renewable energy provider.

Two others who are not on the list but who have made hundreds of millions, if not (yet) billions, are Ethan Brown, the founder of Beyond Meat, the alternative meat company that floated on the stock market in 2019 and attracted huge interest from investors looking to ride the vegan wave; and Patrick Brown (no relation), founder of rival company Impossible Foods.

Some critics argue that there is an inconsistency in the idea of a climate billionaire. People who care about the environment also often believe in social justice and equality. Many billionaires have made their money directly through oil and are now among the leading lobbyists against climate change, a phenomenon prompting *GQ* magazine to argue that 'Billionaires Are the Leading Cause of Climate Change'. Advocates of a wealth tax argue that revenues from such a policy could be funnelled into schemes that would help cut emissions across societies: for example, clean energy and infrastructure projects. When New York billionaire Michael Bloomberg announced that he was donating $500m to a new campaign, Beyond Carbon, which aimed to close every coal-fired power plant in the US, the *Guardian* newspaper argued that philanthropy was nice, but due to the propensity of Bloomberg's billionaire peers to hoard cash and lobby for fossil fuel interests, 'it would be much better for the planet if billionaires like him didn't exist at all'.

But the oil billionaire who lobbies for more fossil fuel extraction is a dying breed. Cynically speaking, those hoping to get rich quick these days are less likely to look to the oil industry to achieve it. As our understanding of risk and climate change evolves, investors are increasingly arguing that it is risky, in ways we may not yet be able to completely measure, to invest in polluting companies, and that the best way to make money in future will be to back climate change solutions and companies that are preparing for a zero-carbon world. While some oil billionaires with the ear of government officials are certainly contributing to climate change, other billionaires like Bloomberg and Bill Gates are actively seeking to mitigate it.

A lot of billionaires do see climate change as a risk. Respondents to the 2020 Global Risks Report, produced in advance of the World Economic Forum in Davos, an annual gathering of some of the world's most influential billionaires and policymakers, listed environmental worries as the five main risks to the global economy – the first time the environment had taken all five top slots. The top three risks were deemed to be extreme weather, climate action failure, and natural disasters – as they had been in 2019 as well.

The boom in wealth

While the push for a low-carbon economy is already creating climate change billionaires in the corporate space, there is also a new wave of wealthy individuals who aren't themselves climate change entrepreneurs but who are looking to invest their money in climate change solutions. Since the global financial crisis of 2008, there has been a boom in wealth. The top 1 per cent have been getting richer, as low interest rates in the past decade incentivised them to invest more, while savers earned less on their money. According to the Knight Frank wealth report, the number of so-called ultra-high-net-worth individuals around the world – those with a net worth of $30m or more – rose by 6.4 per cent in 2019 to 513,200, an extra 31,000 people from the year before alone.

Extreme wealth is helpful when it comes to backing new technologies, as this involves greater risk, though with the potential for greater reward. Some of the most innovative solutions to climate change – emission-friendly meat grown in labs; hydrogen-powered aircraft; eco-friendly air conditioners – are thought up by entrepreneurs and are still only at the start-up stage. Private companies like this depend on early-stage investors, whether venture capitalists in San Francisco, enlightened institutional investors, or high-net-worth individuals looking to back the next big thing.

Some families are so wealthy that they set up family offices. These are investment companies, often with $1bn or more in assets, that have only one client: the family. Think of a billionaire and they are very likely to have their own family office: George Soros has Soros Fund Management; Google founder Sergey Brin has Bayshore Global Management; Bill Gates has Cascade Investments. Many others belong to families that are less well known: the quiet billionaires who made money not through the glamour of Silicon Valley but via industrial or manufacturing routes. And family offices will often have influential younger members – those belonging to the millennial generation, or the generation beyond that, known as Gen Z, who typically care more about the environment. Their influence is helping family offices to be an important class of investors in climate change solutions, as they are in a position to back entre-preneurs.

Titans of tech are also funnelling both philanthropic and investment money into climate change solutions. Jeff Bezos, founder of Amazon, said in February 2020 that he would donate $10bn – about 8 per cent of his wealth at the time – via the newly created Bezos Earth Fund to fight climate change. (The move came shortly after hundreds of Amazon staff signed a letter attacking the company's progress on reducing its carbon foot-print.) In 2015, along with other billionaires including Jack Ma, Richard Branson and Michael Bloomberg, Microsoft founder Bill Gates set up Breakthrough Energy Ventures, an investment fund aimed at support-ing new technologies that could combat climate change.

In short, however one may feel about whether billion-aires should be allowed to exist, they do have a role to play in the energy transition. While a lot of old-school billionaires have contributed to climate change and still lobby in favour of the polluting activities that made them rich, more modern billionaires are trying to use their wealth to help find solutions – though it would probably help their image if they took fewer private jets along the way.

*

In the chapters that follow, we'll look at the different ways in which you can use your money to help combat climate change. We'll discuss emerging trends and controversial areas of investment and demystify the jargon – all of which will empower you with the information you need to make sustainable investment decisions that are right for you.

Throughout the book we'll examine the growing issue of greenwashing, as some investment houses try to seem more climate-friendly than they really are. Some of this can be explained by confusing terms used by the financial industry and a lack of consensus on what is really meant by 'sustainable investing'. By the end of the book, you'll hopefully be able to spot greenwashed investments yourself and work out whether something is clearly labelled, and hence whether you're comfortable investing in it.

First up, in Chapter 2, we'll look at some of the basics of investing, such as how to work out your risk appetite, and why putting your money into what your friends are investing in is probably a bad idea. We'll look at some of the types of investments you can make, from equities to bonds to private equity, and explain how these different ways of investing in companies can give you different kinds of power. We'll look at pensions, as that's where it all begins and ends for a lot of smaller investors. We'll also start to look at greenwashing, and how the financial industry uses acronyms that can be off-putting for those starting out but that shouldn't deter you once you under-stand them.

In Chapter 3, we'll discuss divestment. Often the first port of call for sustainable investors, divestment is the choice not to invest in harmful companies or sectors, most often fossil fuels. We'll consider its benefits and risks, whether it has worked in the past, whether it could harm your investment returns, and how effective it really is at getting companies to reduce their carbon emissions.

In Chapter 4, we'll look at the flip side of divestment, which is engagement with companies. A growing number of investors think that remaining invested in a polluting company gives you more power to effect change than if you divest entirely. We will examine this argument. We'll also look at how investment companies that manage your money are themselves shareholders of the largest companies in the world. These so-called institutional investors have huge clout to push polluting companies to change their ways. And they are increasingly banding together to put pressure on the world's largest companies to do more to combat climate change. Being a climate-conscious investor doesn't necessarily mean disengaging from polluting companies, as we'll discuss.

Chapters 5 to 8 will explore four core themes around climate change investing. Chapter 5, on energy, will look at how governments and energy companies are trying to move away from coal, oil and gas towards renewable energy sources like solar and wind, in what is known as the energy transition. There are plenty of emerging technologies here that you could use your money to support – or you could choose to invest in companies that are positioning themselves well for a low-carbon future.

Chapter 6 looks at the opportunities to invest in green

transport, from electric scooters to biofuelled aero-planes, and at the efforts investors are making to find solutions to the problems of electric batteries still being too heavy, or taking too long to charge. Chapter 7 is all about the food revolution, from the vegan movement and alternative meat to vertical farming and new ways of growing food. Chapter 8 concentrates on energy effi-ciency and the circular economy, and on how even companies not directly helping to solve climate change are making efforts to cut their emissions.

In all these thematic chapters we'll look at some of the high-profile investors backing these ideas, the entre-preneurs coming up with the solutions, and ways that you can get involved, depending on your appetite for risk.

Finally, in the conclusion, we'll look at what still needs to be done by regulators and governments to make it easier for investors both big and small to support cli-mate change solutions. We'll also look at how sustainable investments have held up during the coronavirus pan-demic, and examine the case for building back better.

A note before we begin: it's important to say that this book isn't trying to tell you what to do. It assumes that you want to know more about how to invest with cli-mate change in mind, but it also aims to help you understand the potential risks involved and make informed decisions. In discussing some of the issues, such as whether to divest, whether to engage, relative performance and risks, a balanced view has been sought.

And some reassurance: if you're reading this book,

you probably don't want to feel any more depressed about climate change than you already do. I'm going to spare you the anxiety-inducing statistics, warnings and likely outcomes if the world doesn't get its act together. It's hard to avoid those headlines, and easy to feel powerless in the face of them. So let's assume we all know the science and are happy to place our faith in the 97 per cent of scientists who agree climate change is a thing. The question is: what can investors do about it? Happily, as we will see, the answer is: a lot.

2

Your Green Investing Building Blocks: What You Need to Know

Caroline was at a dinner party when her friend David told her he had been investing in a company that recycled plastic to make products to reuse in other industries. He was retired and had been building up a retirement portfolio after a career in finance. 'I'm helping the environment as well as making money,' he told her. Caroline had a background in campaigning against plastic packaging and loved the idea. She bought £5,000 worth of shares and topped it up with another £3,000 two years later as the company appeared to be doing so well. 'David seemed to be having success generally with his portfolios so I assumed he had made well-researched choices,' she says. 'I did read up about the company, but I invested largely based on his recommendation.'

The company in question was called Environmental Recycling Technologies (ERT). It had found a way of recycling plastics into commercially viable products like building materials. In 2002, ERT listed its shares on London's alternative investment market (AIM) – a stock market mostly comprising smaller companies, which are often more volatile. After losing £2.6m in 2006, the company had predicted it would lose just under £1.7m the next year. It actually lost £4.7m in 2007. But it didn't make this public knowledge until the summer of 2008. Usually companies are expected to warn their shareholders as soon as possible when they've done worse than they expected. In 2009, ERT was publicly censured by the London Stock Exchange after it said it did not communicate these losses properly to its shareholders. The company eventually went bust, and Caroline lost all her money. 'I was devastated,' she says, 'both because of the money and the failure to produce a practical outcome.'

Caroline had also put some money into a fund run by BlackRock called the New Energy Investment Trust. She sat on the board of a local renewable energy charity and one of her colleagues there had been enthusiastic about the fund. The colleague thought it was a good sign that large corporations were beginning to commit to sustainability issues and that this would herald positive growth in the sector. Caroline invested £5,000 in the fund. She did read the marketing material for it first, but says, 'I assumed that anything taken up by BlackRock would be a success.' The fund didn't make much money and Caroline became increasingly frustrated watching the wider stock market power ahead. Eventually she cashed in her investments – losing £110 in total, according to her calculations; a lower loss but still a loss. BlackRock closed the fund in 2014, after a period of underperformance.

Caroline worries that she invested according to her principles but didn't consider the practical side of choosing an investment fund. 'I feel that I was very naïve in investing by word of mouth, but even if I had done more research myself, I would have probably made the same choices,' she says. Her experience also made her doubt whether she should even be trying to invest with the environment in mind. 'This has probably happened to a lot of people like me, so if my investment made no contribution to positive environmental solutions nor any financial gain, what was the point?' she asks.

Caroline's experiences highlight some of the issues that we'll explore in this chapter, with the aim of giving a clear understanding of the different types of investments available and – crucially – who should be investing in them based on their experience and appetite for risk. We'll also look at how different types of investments – equities or bonds, for example – can influence companies' behaviour, as this is an important link when it comes to investing to save the planet. And we'll look at how it's hard to identify funds that are investing in climate change solutions, given a lack of clear labelling in the financial industry. Firstly, though, we'll consider the personal aspect to all investing, whether it's sustainable or not.

Understanding risk

One mistake people can make when wondering what to do with their money is assuming that there are objective choices out there: that there is a right or wrong answer when it comes to managing your finances. There isn't. Friends sometimes ask me what they should do with their money: what fund they should invest in, or even what sort of mortgage they should get. I explain that it depends on what they want to achieve with an investment and how they approach risk. There's a big difference, for example, between someone who invests some spare money in a start-up just to see what happens and someone who needs a steady income to support them in retirement.

Investment decisions are deeply personal to the individual. Financial advisers know this. They will ask you how much risk you want to take, and why you're investing. Do you need an income? How long can you invest the money for? Are you saving for a specific purchase, or for retirement? That's why you shouldn't just copy your friends, as Caroline did with David. The company he was investing in might have made sense for him given his risk portfolio and goals – maybe he had money to burn – but it probably didn't make sense for her. A good financial adviser will suggest investment products or styles that are in line with your financial goals and your risk tolerance.

Investing ethically adds a new layer of personal decisions.

That's because, just as there's no one answer to what investment fund you should buy or what mortgage you should get, there's no one answer for how you should invest to save the planet. Companies and funds that are helping to mitigate climate change are choosing to do it in different ways. Some of their methods you may agree with, and some you may not. It's a personal choice.

This is something you'll probably be familiar with as someone who cares about climate change in your everyday life. If you're trying to reduce your carbon footprint, you will have made certain choices that are personal to you. You may be recycling but not going vegan. You might care strongly about animal welfare but not worry about how frequently you fly. Or you might fly but choose to carbon-offset by planting trees. You may worry that you're being inconsistent, or that you don't have time to do all the research to make the best choice. I frequently wish that there were simple guidelines laid down: if I want to make sustainable fashion choices, for example, I don't want to have to do a huge amount of research. I'd like there to be a one-stop website that listed the brands I should buy. Some research has shown that it's better to buy a fruit that has travelled all the way from the other side of the world than one grown out of season just down the road, with all the energy-guzzling hothousing that entails – but perhaps only if the fruit came by boat and not on a plane. It's not immediately obvious how to work this out when you're standing in a shop looking at tomatoes.

It's even more complicated when it comes to your

investments. One problem is that not all environmental companies are ethical. Do you care more about the environmental damage of polyester in clothing fabric or the way that workers in sweatshops are treated? The same company might not score as highly on both topics. Do you want to invest nothing at all in fossil fuel companies, or would you be happy with those that are investing more than their peers in renewables? If a company was aiming to do great things for the environment by creating electric cars, would you still want to invest in it if it were run by a person who seemed a little unhinged and if it treated its workers badly?

The financial industry does not help itself when it comes to making clear to consumers what they are buying. It has an unhelpful obsession with ugly-sounding acronyms. The financial crisis of 2008 introduced us to the joys of MBSs (mortgage-backed securities) and CDOs (collateralised debt obligations), Libor (London inter-bank offered rate) and Forex (foreign currency). Professional investors these days will even refer to the 'GFC' when talking about the global financial crisis. They just can't help themselves.

In the world of sustainable investing, acronyms like ESG can be interpreted in different ways. A financial adviser will help you to understand some of the terminology. We'll examine some of the uses and interpretations of the terms, but it's worth making one thing clear now: there's no one answer here. You'll have to decide your own interpretation and what matters to you and then you can start making some clearer investment decisions. First we'll look at the sorts of investments you can choose and how these can help you to influence companies or help them grow.

Equities

The way most investors start building a portfolio is through shares in a company, also known as equities. You can buy these directly, or invest in a mutual fund that will hold the shares of lots of different companies. Funds are either active or passive, meaning that there's either an active fund manager who decides which equities to buy, or an automated, passive process. Passive funds are cheaper, because you're not paying for the supposed expertise of the fund manager.

Passive funds have been growing in popularity this century. You may know them as ETFs, or exchange-traded funds. ETFs automatically track a stock market index, such as the MSCI World or the FTSE 100. These indices are just lists of companies: the FTSE 100 lists the 100 biggest listed companies in the UK, for example, while the MSCI World lists 1,644 companies around the world. Some ETFs track indices that have been specially created for ESG companies – or, crucially, what the index provider deems to be ESG companies. It's important to understand that buying any ESG fund, whether passive or active, means you're putting your trust in someone else's definition. And that may not be the same as yours.

The question of whether to buy active or passive funds is highly relevant when it comes to sustainable investing. It has implications not just for retail investors but for institutional investors and the index providers that passive funds track. That's because there's a debate over how far passive investors can influence the companies they own – and we'll return to this in Chapter 4.

Equities are deemed to be, on average, riskier than other types of asset classes, such as bonds, property or cash. They also have the potential for higher returns. For that reason, younger investors, or those investing for the longer term, are usually advised to prioritise – or 'overweight' – equities in their portfolio. But equities are also useful for retired investors who want their investments to pay them an income, as shares pay dividends. Crucial to the climate change investing issue is that fossil fuel companies have historically been among the highest dividend payers. That means they often hold pride of place in income portfolios, and some investors may fear losing that if they switch to sustainable stocks.

Equities come in different shapes and sizes. The bigger a company is, in general, the less risky it is deemed to be. Companies listed on the biggest stock exchanges in the world, like the FTSE 100 in the UK or the S&P 500 in the US, are usually less volatile than smaller companies, which means that their share prices are less likely to fluctuate wildly. Holding equities of smaller companies in your portfolio is, in general, riskier. The UK's small cap index is known as AIM, while the US has the Russell 2000. The company that Caroline bought was an

AIM-listed company; it is very doubtful that this was the right thing for her to do when considering her overall investment portfolio. But it's worth noting that companies whose main purpose is to help reduce carbon emissions are likely to be newer. Therefore, if they're listed, they're probably going to be smaller – and riskier.

As we shall see when we come to our chapter on divestment, there is debate over how far holding a share benefits a company or selling a share harms it: whether to hold certain types of shares may be as much about taking a moral stance as it is about trying to effect change.

Bonds

Bonds are a type of loan that companies or governments use to finance themselves. Government bonds tend to be recommended to balance out equities in a portfolio: when stock markets fall, government bonds from stable countries – particularly the US – tend to rise, as they are seen as a safe haven. Corporate bonds can play a particularly useful role when it comes to climate change investment. One criticism of equities is that they are simply a sliver of a share in a company: owning them doesn't direct your money within that company. But corporate bonds can be used for specific things, and thus can give you greater clarity over how your money is being used. A company might issue a bond with a particular environmental project or purpose in mind, for example.

Green bonds are a mushrooming area of finance for environmentally minded investors. They are issued by companies financing specific projects that should facilitate the transition to a green economy, such as renewable energy, green buildings, clean transportation or energy efficiency. Such companies don't have to be sustainable specialists. Apple, for example, issued a green bond in November 2019 and said it would use that money from investors to develop more energy-efficient and recyclable products and to help cut its suppliers' carbon emissions.

Bond holders also arguably have more clout than equity holders. Big equity investors in a company have a voice, of course. But the worst they can do is sell their shares — and, as we'll see in the next chapter, someone else is usually around to buy them. There is an immediacy to the way a company needs a bond to be refinanced that can focus the mind. Investor group ShareAction says it has spoken to bond holders who refuse to refinance companies they've lent to unless certain conditions are met — for example, unless a company sets science-based targets for its carbon emissions. Many people advocating change through investment say that bonds are better than equities for this reason.

Bonds have a different risk profile to equities. They are unlikely to return as much, though they do provide an income. Their value can be eroded in times of inflation, unlike equities. Also note that few investors, if they are not of the professional stripe, can buy bonds directly, as they can with equities. Minimum investments are too large, and the market is also less liquid, so any bonds in your portfolio are likely to be held through funds. The average retail investor cannot just load up their portfolio with bonds and ignore equities. The traditional advice when investing is to spread risk across various asset classes as well as sectors, on the assumption that they won't all fall in value at once – except in exceptional circumstances, such as the global pandemic experienced in 2020.

Private equity

Private equity investors take a stake in an unlisted company: one that is still private and hasn't floated on the stock market. While equities and bond funds form part of a normal portfolio for an average retail investor, private equity is often only advised for those with more money to invest. This is because it's generally riskier and you often have to commit more money upfront. Investing in private companies that will then either be bought by bigger companies or list themselves on the stock market is the mainstay of private and institutional investors with significant resources. The returns can be a lot higher. Everyone who can afford it wants to be backing the next unicorn (a term for private companies worth over $1bn).

Professional private equity investors are often very active, and this is where it gets interesting for climate change investment. These investors are usually deliberately trying to shape change at the companies they invest in. The business model of a private equity fund is either to buy struggling companies and turn their fortunes around, selling them at a higher price, or to help smaller companies on their journey to list publicly, at which point the private equity investors usually cash out. Nino Tronchetti Provera, head of European private equity company Ambienta, which specialises in environmental investments, says he looks for companies with 'environmental edges': for example, those that may not yet have branched out much beyond their home market. 'We try to make them better companies to take full advantage of those edges globally,' he says.

Companies experimenting with innovative ideas – such as clean energy or alternative meat technology – will probably have private equity investors at a certain stage of their development. Beyond Meat is a great example of this. The alternative meat company went public in May 2019. As a private company, held by private equity investors among others, it had been valued at $1.3bn. But its valuation leapt to $12bn after it listed, as equity investors excited about the prospects for alternative meat were able to snap up shares. Its private equity backers stood to make eye-watering gains: one of them, Mark Yusko at Morgan Creek Capital Management, said his fund's initial investment in Beyond Meat had increased about 100 times.

Private equity investors play a big role in investing in climate change solutions. They are well placed to identify new companies that are trying to innovate. Their investment timescale is also relevant: they are usually looking to make money over at least a five-year period, which gives such companies breathing space to become profitable.

A 2019 report by Coller Capital found that almost three in five private equity investors in Europe and Asia-Pacific planned to modify their portfolios to combat climate change in the next five years – though this fell to less than a third for North American investors. Those that were envisaging changes mainly planned to replace oil and gas exposure with invest-ment in renewable energy and climate-friendly products and services.

The barrier for buying a direct stake in a private equity fund is high: anywhere between $250,000 and $25m. Or you can buy funds of funds (funds that invest in other funds) or listed private equity funds, which are more accessible to retail investors. Bear in mind that these can have layers of extra fees, so you'll need to get a higher return to make it worth it – which private equity funds, in theory, are supposed to achieve.

Venture capital

Venture capital is a subset of private equity and the two terms can overlap. Many of Beyond Meat's private equity backers classed themselves as venture capitalists. Ven-ture capitalists usually invest in companies at an earlier stage than other private equity investors. A start-up that is still experimenting with its technology, for example, would be more likely to ask venture capitalists to invest; private equity investors tend to get involved once it's clear that the technology works and can be produced on a bigger scale. Like private equity funds, barriers to entry are high if you want to invest directly in a venture capital fund. But there are other options: some venture capital funds are listed on a stock market and offer shares to investors. Because venture capital funds are investing at an earlier stage of a company's development, the returns are again usually higher, but the risk is higher too.

Angel investing

Angel investing is a less formalised version of venture capital, and involves individual investors giving money to a start-up. If a friend started a company and asked you to invest, you'd probably be classed as an angel investor. There are certain rules around to protect angel investors, as this is an extremely high-risk form of investment. In the UK, investors have to be classed as high-net-worth individuals – for example, by having an income of at least £100,000 a year. But most new companies, even those that have great ideas, find it hard to make a good idea profitable – or profitable on a wide scale. The rate of failure is extreme: about 90 per cent of angel investments don't make any money at all. That skews the normal rule of investing whereby the riskier something is, the higher returns it will yield. Angel investment is mostly risk with very little prospect of return. But it's exciting and it's understandable why people want to do it: they want to pick the next big thing.

THE ANGEL INVESTOR

Adam Parr, 55, is a former Williams F1 chief executive who is now an angel investor in early-stage companies. He regards finding solutions to climate change as a priority. He and his business partner look for companies at a very early stage in need of money that venture capitalists aren't prepared to give them yet. He says: 'Our investment hypothesis is to go in early to really interesting businesses. We will invest early in the bleeding-edge stage of companies and make fairly big bets early on where we think we can make a difference.' The private sector, Parr believes, 'will play a huge role in the development and deployment of technology'.

One company he invests in is Wirth Research, founded by Nick Wirth, who used to work in Formula 1. The company uses aerodynamic technology to help ventilate office buildings – such as the Apple headquarters in California – without the use of air conditioning or heating. It can also be used in energy-saving refrigeration in shops and fuel-saving aerodynamic systems in trucks such as those used by Royal Mail. Parr says that his interest in such companies was initially driven by the potential for investment returns. But he realised that in a world that is taking climate change seriously, companies helping the world transition to a low-carbon economy were likely to be successful both financially and environmentally. 'I just thought it was a great theme to invest in, but over the last couple of years I must say that my interest in climate change has got much more serious,' he says. 'There's no question that we are in an energy transition and we are going to be decarbonising the global economy, so companies looking in that field are obviously investing in the grain.'

Pensions

The reality is that many retail investors may have limited choice over where they can invest their money. That is because, for most people, their main investment is their pension. Many people will hold a pension through a workplace scheme, which will match contributions or even double them. Your workplace will typically have selected a fund manager to manage its pensions. In modern types of corporate pension, known as defined contribution pensions in the UK, this fund manager will offer a selection of funds, no more than a handful, and you can choose which one you'd like to put your pension savings into. There is often one ethical choice. Remember that this might not be environmental: 'ethical' is a wide umbrella term that could mean any company that has decent governance, or is treating workers well. It might have nothing to do with climate change.

If you don't say which fund you want, you're put into the default fund – which almost certainly won't be an ethical one. This is likely to be a long-lasting choice: in the UK, more than 90 per cent of people never bother to switch out of the default fund. But there is nothing stopping you from swapping funds, so it's definitely worth looking at your options.

Most people don't think about their company pension fund as something they have much control over. But this is expected to change. Encouraging consumers to think about where their pension money is invested is the latest campaign of Richard Curtis, the UK film director behind *Four Weddings and a Funeral* and *Love Actually*, who is now a UN advocate for the sustainable development goals. He recalls watching a TED talk by Bronwyn King, an oncologist who discovered that her investment funds had holdings in tobacco companies, and realising that people's 'financial footprint' is even more important than changes in their lifestyle as a consumer. His Make My Money Matter movement is aimed at encouraging pension holders and savers to push their money into sustainable investments and engage with their employers to do the same with their pension funds. 'The most powerful thing people can do in their lives is check where their investment is going,' he says.

Lifting the lid on climate funds

Many people reading this book will have money to invest beyond their pension, and their first port of call is likely to be a fund, whether active or passive. When you're building up an investment portfolio, it is likely to include equities and bonds, and perhaps, depending on your risk level and wealth, private equity or even venture capital funds too. There are green or sustainable versions of all these asset classes. Yet trying to find a climate change fund is currently quite a confusing task. Climate change investing is still in its infancy. It's hard to say what a climate change fund actually is – and fund data providers like Morningstar don't yet have a specific category for such funds. There's a lack of standardisation and consistency across the industry in general that can cause confusion when it comes to investing with the environment in mind. Fund managers may not be deliberately trying to mislead or greenwash with a particular product. Different terms may just mean different things to different people. That's why it's important to understand how the terms can be used. While it helps to look at the names of funds and strategies when considering what investment product to buy, investors may need to go the extra mile themselves and consider whether the product is really doing what they would like or expect it to.

As we've seen, the Paris Agreement of 2015 and the publication of the UN Sustainable Development Goals was a catalyst for the fund management industry, heralding an explosion in new options for investors. Because there has been such a leap for the bandwagon, many climate change funds are very recent, making their performance record hard to assess: in the financial industry, a track record of at least three if not five years is usually standard before one can say anything meaningful about how a fund has performed relative to its peers. But we can look at what is inside a lot of these funds, which we'll explore in subsequent chapters.

In April 2020, Morningstar published a report that noted a recent surge in the number of climate-aware funds, with 76 new ones in 2019 following 67 the previous year (its analysis was based on Europe only). In addition to those new funds, many existing conventional or more broadly 'sustainable' funds either changed their mandate to focus on the climate theme, or added specific climate-related criteria to their investment policy.

In an attempt to shape the climate change funds landscape for investors, Morningstar in 2020 divided what it called 'climate-aware funds' into six main groups: low carbon, ex-fossil fuel, climate conscious, climate solutions, green bond, and clean energy/tech. We'll look at these groups in the coming chapters, as some of the funds are more appropriate for the various investment strategies we'll be exploring when it comes to climate change investing.

The difference between the climate-aware funds out there highlights the importance for investors of doing their homework before selecting a fund, ideally using a financial adviser to help them sift through the various options and looking at the holdings of each fund to make sure they are comfortable with them and understand the strategy being used by the fund manager. In general, investors should check the top 10 holdings of a fund – the only holdings a fund is required to publish – to get an idea of what sort of things it includes.

There are of course other things you can do with your money when it comes to combating climate change that we won't consider as investing in the strict sense for the purposes of this book. There is crowdfunding – probably closest to angel investing in spirit – where people with new ideas can raise money on a website. There's charitable giving or philanthropy, which is certainly a crucial tool in combating climate change but not strictly speaking an investment. Then there's impact investment, a newer area whereby funds or projects try to measure their impact. Impact investment spans a broad area that can include philanthropy, investing for a below-market return, or investing for a normal return. We'll see some examples of this later in the book, but it won't be a primary focus.

As we discuss investment themes in the following chapters, we'll look at different ways of investing in them that will include the asset classes we've looked at here, whether equities, bonds, private equity or venture capital. Where specific funds are mentioned, these are just examples of some of the options out there. It doesn't constitute investment advice: as this chapter has hopefully demonstrated, getting financial advice is a personal thing, akin to having a good therapist, so anyone thinking of investing in a particular fund or company should consult a professional and make sure it's the right thing for them.

What can you do?

- The first thing you should do if you're thinking about adjusting your investment portfolio, or investing for the first time, is to talk to a financial adviser. They don't have to be a climate change investment specialist but they should be familiar with ESG investing in general.
- Make sure they take the time to discuss your needs with you and adjust their advice accordingly. Do your homework on what sort of climate change investing suits you so you can go to the meeting armed with some knowledge: a task that will become easier once you've read the following chapters.
- Check your company pension and where your money is invested. Are you in the default fund, and are you happy with that? Is there an ethical option?

3

Running Out of Gas: Does Divestment Work?

In 2014, a letter landed in an office on the leafy campus of Georgetown University in Washington DC. The office belonged to Michael Barry, chief investment officer for the college endowment fund. It was from a group of undergraduate students who were calling on the university to ditch its holdings in fossil fuels because of concerns over climate change. The Georgetown students were riding a recent wave of student activism on fossil fuel divestment across US colleges. The movement had started in 2010, after students on the small campus of Swarthmore College in Pennsylvania visited the nearby Appalachian Mountains and witnessed the environmental and social effects of mountaintop removal by the coal companies.[*]

---

[*] Mountaintop removal involves using explosives to blow off the top of a mountain to get at the coal inside. The resulting air pollution has been linked to health issues in local communities.

The students were stunned by what they saw, and began a campaign to persuade their college to ditch its investments in the fossil fuel industry. Other college campuses joined in, and in 2011, Hampshire College became the first in the US to divest its college endowment fund from fossil fuels.

When the letter from his students arrived, Barry began researching the investment case for Georgetown to do the same. In 2015, he and his team decided to exit coal companies, and in February 2020, Georgetown made global headlines as it became one of the most prominent universities in the world to announce it was divesting from oil and gas. 'One of the most important components was studying the financial implications,' Barry says. 'It seemed divestment had potentially positive effects. Our net conclusion was it wouldn't hurt the endowment and it could even benefit it.'

Georgetown University is the latest participant in the now global divestment movement that has seen many college endowment funds, city pension funds and even whole countries announce their intention to sell their fossil fuel investments. The climate change action group 350.org, which was founded in 2009 by a group of university students and now advocates for divestment from fossil fuels, says that since Hampshire College took the first step back in 2011, over a thousand institutions have followed suit. In 2018, Ireland became the world's first country to announce it was selling the coal, oil and gas holdings in its state-owned national investment fund. The same year, New York City said it planned to divest from its fossil fuel holdings within five years. These actions have understandably been hailed as a great step forward for investment in the climate change era. As more investors think about the use to which their money is being put, the argument goes, polluting companies will suffer and carbon dioxide emissions will become lower.

There is just one small problem. Divestment may not work.

A socially responsible history

To understand why investors have started divesting from fossil fuels and what they are trying to achieve by doing so, it's helpful to look at this movement in the longer-term context of socially responsible investment.

Thinking about the social and moral implications of your money is not something unique to the modern world. People have been pondering it for hundreds if not thousands of years. The Bible teaches: 'Better is a little with righteousness than vast revenues without justice' (Proverbs 16:8). The Quran forbids Muslims from making a profit on interest, and Sharia-compliant investment funds – which hold billions on behalf of Muslims around the world – avoid investments in things deemed to be unethical, such as gambling and tobacco.

The modern socially responsible investment movement is often traced back to the eighteenth century, when a group of American Quakers took the decision to divest themselves completely from the slave trade. The Quakers of London soon followed, and in 1787, they helped to form the Society for Effecting the Abolition of the Slave Trade. Their divestment strategy of avoiding an investment they found to be morally troubling, coupled with campaigning to bring awareness to the problem, had an impact and helped to bring about the eventual abolition of the slave trade in the British Empire in 1807.

During apartheid in South Africa in the 1970s and 80s, student union and religious groups began campaigning for multinational companies with business activities in South Africa to pull out of a country that still segregated black and white people. In the UK, the National Union of Students put particular pressure on Barclays Bank, with their 'Don't Bank on Apartheid' campaign. In 1986, Barclays sold its South African arm. It claimed that the decision had been largely a commercial one, because profits had been falling at the unit. But executives admitted that it had also been due to the growing pressure around the world against the South African government. 'World opinion counts,' Sir Timothy Bevan, then the chairman of Barclays, told the *New York Times*. 'It affects commerce. And world opinion has changed quite a lot this year.'

What these movements had in common is that, whether for religious, political or moral reasons, investors have historically tended to avoid certain areas when investing with their conscience. This avoidance can come in the form of either negative screening or divestment. Negative screening involves avoiding making any new investments in certain types of company, for example coal or tobacco; while divestment involves selling investments in those companies that were bought at some point when they were deemed to be less controversial.

Most investors who care about the environment start by thinking about what they *don't* want to invest in. Julian Parrott, an independent financial adviser who runs an ethical investment practice in Edinburgh, says that by far the most common thing new clients state at the start of the conversation is that they want to avoid investing in fossil fuels. A 2016 survey by UK-based fund manager Schroders found that 32 per cent of millennials would divest themselves of any investment they had made in a company that was contributing negatively to climate change, even if it was performing well – compared to 26 per cent of those over the age of 36.

Feeling uncomfortable about investing in polluting companies is understandable. We often avoid things we don't approve of: this doesn't apply only to investments, but also to products we consume, holidays in places with dodgy regimes, the type of company we work for, and even friendships and the people we associate with. But does it make financial sense?

Some people take the view that they don't care how profitable Shell is or how much income its shares would provide them with in retirement: if it's damaging the planet, they don't want to profit from that personally.

They're happy to make less money as a result. But will they?

Others have a different aim in mind: they take the view that their divestment will ultimately harm Shell or have a negative impact on the fossil fuel industry. But will it? We'll explore both of these questions in this chapter.

'Divestment has reduced zero tonnes of emissions'

Some people naturally think that if lots of investors sell their shares in an oil and gas company, then the share price will fall and the company will begin to struggle. The falling share price would in theory affect its ability to buy other companies or get a loan from a bank and so damage its prospects in other ways.

Share prices of companies often rise and fall based on sentiment. People devote their careers to rigorous stock market analysis based on fundamental financial metrics, but psychology plays a huge role too. Yet while there are instances of companies becoming unloved because of investor sentiment towards them, we are not yet in a world where an oil and gas company is likely to go out of business because nobody is buying their shares any more. That is because – for now, at least – there are always buyers without scruples. A 2018 article in the *Wall Street Journal* argues: 'The trouble is, even badly run companies, big polluters or terrible employers have some price at which they will be profitable investments.' If the share price falls low enough, some people will spot a bargain. You might argue that this is defeatist – the same as saying that there is no point recycling if your neighbours don't bother. Yet we are very far from a world where investors will always put morals before profit. Financial markets look for inefficiencies, in both the short and long term. If fossil fuel companies appear undervalued, it would be naïve to think nobody would try to profit from that.

Even people looking to divest are usually pragmatic about it. Michael Barry at Georgetown says that one reason they have given themselves five years to get out of their holdings in oil and gas is that they think the sector could rebound a little in coming years, so they don't want to sell at the bottom of the market. The fact that someone else will probably buy oil and gas company shares if they fall low enough and make a profit is sometimes cited as a reason why investing in climate change solutions means giving up on returns.

Despite campaigners for divestment movements claiming victory, there is no conclusive evidence that divestment directly hurts share prices. Some argued, for example, that the end of apartheid was at least in part due to boycotts of South African companies and the financial pain they felt as a result. A paper by economists in the 1990s noted the relatively recent trend towards divestment in areas like tobacco and oil and gas companies – in 1990, Harvard University ditched tens of millions of dollars' worth of tobacco stocks, for example – and decided to research whether the boycotts in South Africa had worked from a financial perspective. They concluded that they had not: 'We find no support for the common perception – and often vehement rhetoric in the financial media – that the anti-apartheid shareholder and legislative boycotts affected the financial sector adversely.'

Bill Gates believes that climate activists are wasting their time lobbying investors to ditch fossil fuel stocks, telling the *Financial Times* in 2019: 'Divestment, to date, probably has reduced about zero tonnes of emissions.' He believes investors who want to change the world should instead be putting their money behind disruptive technologies that slow carbon emissions, which is something that his fund, Breakthrough Energy Ventures, is currently doing.

The economic case for divestment

It is hard to prove that divestment has an immediate financial impact on a company in the short term. But the direction of causation increasingly looks as though it's going the other way: divestment may make more sense as a financial reaction to climate change. Investors increasingly believe that stricter regulations and consumer sentiment will ultimately harm the fossil fuel industry – and, crucially, harm their investment returns over the long term. In the coal industry, for example, the economic case for divestment has been clearer than for oil and gas companies as the companies are higher polluters and have less chance of pivoting their business to renewables. Coal divestment has taken place at a large scale as regulation has also hit returns. This offers a glimpse of what the future could hold for oil and gas companies. A 2015 report by Carbon Tracker examined the coal market in the US and found that, due to a combination of increased regulation and lower prices for alternative fuels such as renewables and shale gas, over two dozen coal companies had gone bankrupt in the previous three years, with others losing over 80 per cent of their share value. This doesn't mean that divestment harmed coal companies' share prices. But it does suggest that divesting is sometimes a financially sensible reaction.

Oil and gas companies also have a specific regulation-driven nightmare: that of stranded assets. Companies like Exxon, BP and Shell are currently sitting on huge reserves of oil and gas, but government regulation aimed at keeping carbon emissions down could mean that they can never use them. A *Financial Times* analysis in February 2020 found that the value of these lost assets could be as high as $900bn – the equivalent of a third of the value of the big oil and gas companies. That gives investors a further economic reason to divest over the long term.

Oil and gas companies are certainly worried. In its 2018 annual report, Shell noted the emergence of the divestment movement and admitted that, if it continued as it had, it could have 'a material adverse effect' on both the company's share price and its ability to access equity capital markets.

If investors choose to divest for longer-term economic

reasons, rather than primarily due to a moral stance, this also turns one of the main arguments against divestment on its head: that it can harm your investment returns. We saw this when David Blood's colleagues at Goldman Sachs laughed at him for moving into sustainable investment. The general rule of thumb in investment theory is that spreading your risk across as many sectors and asset classes as possible is the best strategy. Some investors worry that restricting your investment universe – by cutting out fossil fuel companies, for example – could harm your financial returns. This has been a particular issue for pension funds, whose trustees are required to maximise returns. Some have interpreted this to mean that they can't ignore oil and gas companies, however polluting they may be.

It's easy to find examples of ethically or environmentally unsound companies that have made plenty of money. In 2019, it was calculated that the company which had made investors most money during the 35-year life of the UK's FTSE 100 index was British American Tobacco.* In 2018, BAT was one of the top five highest dividend payers in the country – and that was despite a long divestment campaign against it. Trustees might point to such research and argue that, as their remit is purely financial, it is not their job to campaign as the Quakers did for societal change.

---

* Research from brokers AJ Bell found that if you bought £100 worth of BAT shares in 1984 and reinvested the dividends, by the beginning of 2019 they were worth £33,123.

But a new interpretation is emerging, as the longer-term risks of climate change become clear. Climate-conscious investors argue that companies whose activities harm the environment are ultimately also harming the members of the pension scheme. That could be in indirect ways, by contributing to a less stable society; or it could be in the longer-term financial ways that we discussed above. The business models of the oil and gas companies will not survive for ever, even if they continue to make money in the short term. There is already evidence that their record as excellent dividend payers is under threat. In April 2020, Royal Dutch Shell – the best dividend payer in the FTSE 100 – cut its dividend for the first time since the Second World War, due to the oil price slump caused by the coronavirus lockdowns. Analysts had already been warning that oil and gas companies were going to become less profitable due to climate change, prompting the *Financial Times* to argue that concerns would only mount over the role of Big Oil investment portfolios.

When Michael Barry was considering whether to divest fossil fuels in Georgetown's endowment fund, one of his main concerns was the risks involved – both in getting out of fossil fuels and in staying invested in them. His research led him to decide that, while the global economy will require oil and gas for some time, the business case for companies whose main gig is to extract oil and gas from the ground and pump it into the atmosphere will only become more challenging. 'We can't predict when regulation or taxation will rise in this industry,' he says, 'but if they do, they're most likely to be negative.'

In general, studies on the statistical likelihood that sustainable investment leads to an underperforming portfolio usually conclude that it does not. A report from Arabesque Asset Management analysed 200 academic studies in this area and discovered that 80 per cent of them found that companies with stronger environmental, social and governance practices had stronger-performing share prices. The report also found a direct relationship between the environmental performance of companies and their stock price performance.

A report from the London Stock Exchange in 2019 looking at the move towards green finance argued that the green economy was actually outperforming the conventional economy – pointing to a 41.1 per cent rise in the FTSE Environmental Opportunities All Share index in the preceding five years versus a 33.4 per cent rise in the FTSE Global All Cap index. And a report in October 2019 from the International Monetary Fund (IMF) found that there was 'no conclusive evidence in the literature that sustainable funds consistently out- or underperform conventional funds'.

Of course, fluctuations in oil prices can easily lead to outperformance of conventional funds against their anti-fossil fuel counterparts, and investors should be prepared for that. But some may not even mind: a study of over 2,000 US investors in October 2019 by the University of Cambridge Institute for Sustainability Leadership that put the participants into real investment situations found a 'strong preference' for sustainable investing even when returns of up to 2–3 per cent were sacrificed.

A paper in 2016, 'The Financial Impact of Divestment from Fossil Fuels', looked at the impact of taking fossil fuels out of an investment portfolio, noting as a starting point that fossil fuel investments had outperformed other investments between 1980 and 2015 and considering the argument that avoiding them would lead to a less diverse portfolio. The study found that a key reason the fossil fuel investments had done better was that they were riskier – higher risk often leading to higher returns – but that on a risk-adjusted basis, 'divesting from fossil fuels does not have a statistically significant impact on overall portfolio performance', with the conclusion: 'The policy implication is that investors can divest from fossil fuels without significantly hurting their financial performance.'

Some will argue it is relevant to the performance debate that fossil fuel companies had higher returns in this study because they were riskier. In a world where their business model is no doubt going to get riskier still, with the threat of more regulation and consumer backlash, they may make money for investors who are prepared to buy them at cheaper levels – a point made by the *Wall Street Journal*.

Fossil fuel companies will no doubt continue to be a profitable investment for a certain period of time. The problem is that, while people agree that the risks they will face are increasing, nobody knows exactly by how much, and how to measure them accurately. Companies are under pressure to assess the risks of climate change to their business themselves, but this is not yet universally required. In 2015, the Financial Stability Board, an international body that monitors the global financial system, set out plans for companies to tell their investors about the financial risks that climate change posed to their business, as part of its Task Force for Climate-Related Financial Disclosures (TCFD). So far, this is a voluntary programme, but a majority of leading banks, asset managers, pension funds and others have signed up to it.

Trying to work out a reasonable way of assessing the risk of companies operating in the fossil fuel sector – or any other area likely to struggle in a world of greater regulation and awareness of climate change – is one of the hot debates at present, which we will return to in the conclusion.

The broad argument is that a fossil fuel company will be – and probably already is – a much riskier prospect as an investment over the medium and longer term. So by avoiding putting your money in these companies and investing elsewhere, you could make more money over the longer term. In 2019, the *Wall Street Journal* called the fall of Californian utility PG&E after wildfires ravaged the US state 'the first climate-change bankruptcy' – and warned it was unlikely to be the last. The IMF report in October said that 'Financial risks from climate change are extremely difficult to quantify, but most studies point to very large economic and financial costs.'

We'll look more at the investment case for energy

companies in Chapter 5. Suffice to say that some pension fund trustees already believe that investing in fossil fuel companies is not a good long-term investment strategy and that it could actually lead people to have a lower income in retirement.

Another area where divestment can have an effect is on the pool of investors willing to invest in oil and gas companies. Investments can become more or less risky depending on how liquid they are: how quickly you can buy or sell them. Having a large market of potential buyers for shares improves liquidity and reduces risk. If fewer people want to buy oil and gas stocks, that will make them less liquid over time. Michael Barry argues: 'The act of people like us divesting in itself creates a headwind for the share prices. You could have a situation where they [oil and gas companies] are value traps – they look cheap, but the buyer set has shrunk so the financial risk to us of owning these companies is rising, especially when you compare it to other sectors of the economy.'

In short, while there is still no clarity over just how risky fossil fuel companies will be in the future, making it possible that they will make investors money for some time to come, the research in general suggests both that investors don't have to give up portfolio performance if they avoid them, and that the risks in the long term may be substantial. That helps to answer the question as to whether it makes financial sense to avoid fossil fuel companies. The answer is that, in the long term, it probably does.

Divesting from fossil fuel producers may not cause direct financial harm to the companies, since other investors, for now at least, will probably step in to buy their shares. But there is another way to hurt them: through public shaming. As divestment campaigns lead to heightened awareness of the need for polluting companies to take climate change more seriously, this can push them to make changes to their business models, for example by investing more in renewable energy or speeding up their transition away from fossil fuels.

It can be argued that the real effect of a public campaign to divest comes through bad publicity – though this is harder to quantify. Writing in the *New Yorker* in 2015, Oxford philosophy professor William MacAskill concluded that divestment campaigns 'have the potential to do good, but only with caveats. To avoid the risk of misleading people, those running campaigns should be clear that the aim of divestment is to signal disapproval of certain industries, not to directly affect share price.'

Michael Barry notes that when Georgetown made its announcement about divesting from fossil fuels in February 2020, the media response was huge. One of the motives for divesting, he says, was to increase awareness, which he feels they succeeded in doing.

Sometimes publicly embarrassing companies has a positive effect. UK fund manager Legal & General

Investment Management (LGIM) named and shamed various companies in its Climate Impact Pledge report in 2018, praising the winners and ditching the losers from its portfolios, which are stacked with billions belonging to pension funds and retail investors. The companies it ousted for not taking ESG considerations seriously enough included China Construction Bank, Dominion Energy and Rosneft Oil. Director of corporate governance at LGIM Sacha Sadan later said that those companies had got in touch with him to ask what they needed to do to be included in LGIM's funds again.

In February 2020, the investment community was left reeling in shock after US money manager and well-known TV pundit Jim Cramer said on CNBC that he was 'done' with fossil fuels. 'We're in the death knell phase,' he said, to the excitement of many in the sustainable investment community. 'We're starting to see divestment all over the world.' He argued that divestment was the biggest factor holding back oil company share prices, saying that even though their dividends were still substantial, the world had turned on them. 'This has to do with new kinds of money managers who frankly just want to appease younger people who believe that you can't ever make a fossil fuel company sustainable . . . It's a new world. Exxon could report an upside surprise and I don't think it would matter.'

The answer to the question of whether divestment will have a negative impact on the fossil fuel industry is therefore also yes: not in the financial sense one might expect, but through public shaming and world opinion.

So if you want to ditch fossil fuels, what should you do? Morningstar has identified two types of mutual funds, low carbon and ex-fossil fuel, which it reckons may appeal to investors who want to decarbonise their port-folios. Remember that the case for divestment can be made on moral grounds – you don't want to personally profit from any oil and gas companies – or performance grounds – you believe that oil and gas companies are going to struggle in a world that is reorienting itself towards climate change mitigation.

Yet even by picking an ex-fossil fuel fund, you may not be avoiding oil and gas companies altogether. Morning-star calculates that only 40 per cent of ex-fossil fuel funds are actually fossil fuel free, due to varying definitions of fossil fuel exclusions. Most of the commonly held com-panies in ex-fossil fuel funds have a low or negligible carbon risk, according to a carbon risk rating created by Sustainalytics, an ESG research and ratings provider. That measurement of carbon risk is not simply the com-pany's carbon footprint: it includes what actions the company is taking to be more sustainable. That helps to explain why some of these commonly held companies are perhaps not obviously in line with what climate-conscious investors want to invest in. They include H&M, a clothing company typically associated with fast fashion, but which has been making efforts to improve its practices more recently. They also include Microsoft, which took the unusual step in January 2020 of announcing not only that it would ensure it was carbon neutral by 2030, but that by 2050 it would have offset all its historical carbon emissions since its founding in 1975.

Another area of confusion, which highlights the importance of researching funds before buying them, is that not all funds will make their low-carbon or ex-fossil fuel status clear in their title, which seems like a missed marketing opportunity given the huge investor interest in such types of funds. For example, while the Amundi IS Equity Europe Low Carbon fund has a clear label, it is not obvious from the name of the Dimensional Global Sustainable Core Equity that it is also targeting low-carbon investments.

THE DISRUPTOR

Jeremy Oppenheim was a partner at McKinsey, the global consulting firm, when he had his light-bulb moment. He had taken a year's sabbatical to head up a project for the Global Commission on the Economy and Climate, an international initiative that analyses and communicates the economic risks and opportunities that arise from climate change. He was looking at whether global economic growth was necessarily in conflict with climate action, and concluded that in many cases it was not. But it was clear that in order to really tackle climate change *and* hold on to economic growth, the global economy would require a major systematic change.

Oppenheim decided that this couldn't be done from within McKinsey, which, though 'brilliant at optimising systems', was not the sort of place that brought about systemic change. 'That was quite wrenching as I was feeling quite happy at McKinsey, but when you learn something, it's very hard to unlearn it and this was one of those moments,' he says. Instead, he founded Systemiq, which is a cross between an adviser to governments and companies and an early-stage investor in new start-ups. It also helps to set up NGOs where it feels they are needed. He says it is hard for some companies to accept that the world is changing and their products might be obsolete – for example, German car manufacturers that have perfected the internal combustion engine having to switch to electric.

Oppenheim admits it is hard to know how the effects of the coronavirus lockdowns of 2020 will play out. On the one hand, companies might try to be more resilient for future shocks and governments could prioritise green recovery programmes, but on the other, people could be desperate to get back to normal and won't have the financial resources to worry about the long-term climate crisis. But he is inclined to view the massive behavioural shifts as an opportunity: 'I tend to believe this is a period in which we will see accelerated creative destruction with winner and loser effects.

I think you'll see the smart money and talent moving to where the future seems to be.'

The divestment debate outside of equities

So far, much of our discussion has focused on divesting
from equities. But a growing number of investors think
that divestment has far more effect if it takes place in
other asset classes, like bonds. They take the view, discussed earlier in this chapter, that divestment won't
harm share prices, but go one step further, believing
that more concrete action needs to be taken in other
asset classes. Cambridge University, for example, has
not divested its £8bn endowment fund despite plenty of
pressure to do so from students and faculty members
alike. Dr Ellen Quigley, an adviser on responsible investment to the university's chief financial officer, argues
that divestment from public equity – in shares that anyone can buy and sell – is a waste of time when it comes
to affecting company behaviour. Worse than that, she
argues, it can be harmful. Most divestment, she says,
only concerns share portfolios rather than other asset
classes, so it can be little more than a box-ticking
exercise for trustees to feel that they have done their
environmental due diligence. She warns: 'Divestment
concentrates on public equity on the secondary market
which doesn't matter as the company already raised the
money. Very few funds apply divestment to other asset

classes where it matters – so we're just rearranging deck-chairs on the *Titanic*. People think job done and don't think about it any more: it actually keeps people from being useful so it's worse than nothing.'

This is a widely held view. 'The most direct impact an investor can make is to invest in green infrastructure of some kind,' says Mark Fulton, chair of the research council at think tank Carbon Tracker. 'That can be achieved by capital recycling from high-carbon to low-carbon across asset classes.' James Purcell, head of ESG at Quintet, a Swiss private bank, says: 'All these companies issued their capital decades ago and as retail investors we just move around pieces of paper that were issued decades ago. We're merely passing it around in a circle.'

The asset class where it really matters, Quigley believes, is the bond market. There are other ways to harm a company financially beyond selling its shares, and a key way is to cut off its access to financing. If nobody will give you a mortgage, you can't buy a house. If an oil and gas company can't get funding for its new project to drill in the Arctic, the project won't take place.

There are two main ways of cutting off a company's access to funding: through the banks, which provide loans to companies; and through the bond market.

Like equities, bonds can be bought and sold in the secondary market, but crucially, companies (and governments) are in constant need of loans so often will issue bonds quite regularly. 'Bonds are a much more targeted way of following money through and identifying what the money being spent will do, for example in local economies,' says the aptly named Simon Bond, director of responsible investment at Columbia Threadneedle, who spent most of his career as a bond fund manager. Quigley says that while Cambridge University itself hasn't divested, around a third of its colleges have. She and some of the bursars of those colleges have met with the university's fund manager to demand that they align their bonds with sustainable principles rather than choosing to finance new projects that would increase emissions. Some have also written to their banks to ask them to stop lending to fossil fuel companies or utility companies that run off coal. 'That's among the more impactful things you can do,' she says.

The next chapter, on positive investment, will look more at these green bonds, as well as the emerging class of transition bonds, but when thinking about divestment, ShareAction's Christian Wilson says that investors should consider what the 'brown' – i.e. conventional – bonds they might hold are financing. A standard bond fund might be helping to finance all sorts of projects that are not climate change-friendly.

While the divestment movement has grown massively in recent years, it is still a minority activity. Mainstream universities like Harvard in the US and Oxford and Cambridge in the UK have historically resisted calls to divest their portfolios. The vast majority of pension funds and institutional investors still put money into fossil fuel companies. Part of the reason for this is that the case for divestment in the short term, as we've discussed, is not as clear-cut as it might seem, even for people concerned about climate change. But many investors concerned about climate change also believe it is more fruitful to engage positively with companies they're invested in, and that will be the topic of our next chapter – whether it makes sense to engage with companies instead, and effect change from within.

What can you do?

- Consider whether you want to divest your investments from fossil fuel stocks altogether (before making this decision, it will be helpful to read the next chapter, on engagement).
- Think about your own mindset, and whether you're prepared to give up some performance in the short term if you do divest: could you stomach seeing oil and gas companies pay out bumper dividends in the next couple of years? Could you afford to miss out on that income?
- Consider buying low-carbon or ex-fossil fuel funds, but be aware that some of these funds may still hold oil and gas stocks. Check the top 10 holdings before you buy and make sure you're comfortable with what the fund is aiming to do.
- Consider whether it makes sense for you to divest from other asset classes as well as equities: are there any bond funds in your portfolio invested in companies that are harming the environment?

4

Fighting the Big Polluters from Within: Engagement and Effecting Change

When Jenny Edwards retired from full-time work at the age of 64, she found herself with spare time on her hands. She had never been particularly interested in personal finance: her career had been in the public sector. Most of her friends simply had a public sector pension and thought no further about financial matters. Her situation was a bit different. Before she retired, she had inherited shares in 10 different companies, including Shell and Marks & Spencer. Until now, those holdings had just ticked along, giving her a regular but very modest income. But now she began to think about where her money was going given her concerns about climate change. Should she sell her shares?

Jenny was used to public speaking. She had been the chief executive of two charities, Homeless Link and the Mental Health Foundation, and had been awarded a CBE for her work. Those roles had seen her sit face to face with UK government ministers, trying to convince them to do things differently. She decided to use her skills of persuasion to convince companies to do more for the environment.

Jenny arrived at the Shell annual general meeting with prepared notes but threw them aside so that she could speak from the heart. 'I wanted to get in early before they were in defensive mode as everybody had been having a go at them. I sat right at the front by the microphone. I think I was the third to speak.' She made three requests: that the company improve the climate expertise of the directors on the board; that they change their investment plans and stop prioritising searching for new fossil fuels; and that they stop lobbying against environmental regulations that would interfere with profit-making. She stressed that, like others in the room, she relied on her dividends, but she argued: 'If I was asked, do I put my family first or do I put my dividends first, there is absolutely no competition: my family, my community, my country, my world, my planet, they all come before my dividends, and I think many people in this room will feel the same.'

The room cheered. Afterwards, the chairman of the Shell board spoke to her at length. 'They really wanted me to believe that they were aware of these things and, as they saw it, at the forefront of their sector.' She knows that her intervention alone may not have changed much. One of the directors sent her something from the communications department that had 'very debatable' ideas in it. 'Obviously my aspirations are for them to go a lot further and faster and deeper but the dialogue is open,' she says. Interestingly, Jenny was speaking before Shell announced in April 2020 that it was introducing a net zero emissions target even amid huge financial pressures from the coronavirus pandemic.

Emboldened, Jenny then went to the Marks & Spencer annual general meeting. AGMs are notorious for having a certain class of retired investor rock up to hear their own opinions and sample the free tea and biscuits. She knew that a long line of these regulars would want to get their questions in first – which tend to be the same every year – and the directors took their time answering. But she had prepared. She wore a bright top – 'I always do, so people can find me in a crowd' – and had made friends with the security people holding the microphones. One of them noticed her and she was the last to speak. She had decided that the company's use of packaging should be singled out. It was 2019, and even then, as now, single fruits or vegetables were often wrapped in plastic. She had brought along a sprig of rosemary wrapped in plastic packaging with 'Morocco' stamped on it to make her point. 'I waved it around when I spoke and said: "This is the kind of thing I'm talking about. Do we not grow rosemary in this country? I grow it in my back garden!"'

The chairman, Archie Norman, told her he agreed with her completely, while another director rushed down from the platform to point out the various measures M&S were taking to improve their packaging situation, including shifting to pots of living herbs that could be sourced in the UK, and training staff in stacking unwrapped fruit and vegetables so that they lasted longer.

While engagement would seem to be the opposite of divestment, the two movements often have similar aims: to change the behaviour of the company. Jenny Edwards's speeches at the Shell and M&S AGMs are an example of this: rather than sell her shares, she chose to use the access to the directors that her shares gave her to talk to them directly. Many professional investors believe that this is the best path forward when it comes to encouraging companies to improve their carbon footprint. We saw in the last chapter that one risk of divestment is that another, less scrupulous investor is likely to buy your shares. That could mean you're handing the company a less engaged shareholder on a platter. 'If you sell something and somebody else buys it, you're just transferring your interest to some-one who cares less than you do. So, it can lead to worse moral outcomes than sitting at the table trying to get things to change,' argues Cameron Hepburn, a profes-sor of environmental economics at the University of Oxford.

Yet you might wonder whether the positive response

Jenny reported from her meetings with the board directors was because she was quizzing them publicly on a trendy topic. Maybe they didn't want to sound as if they didn't care about climate change. Do board directors really listen to the views of their smallest shareholders? Can retail investors effect real change?

If investors work together, their chances are improved. ShareAction, a UK-based shareholder group focusing on environmental, social and governance change at companies, offers training for individual members on how to ask constructive rather than aggressive questions at AGMs in a way that, it argues, can help members build good relationships with the board over the years.

It also pools its members to file calls for action at companies. In the UK, just 100 shareholders with £100 worth of shares each are needed to file a resolution. In January 2020, ShareAction filed the first ever climate-related shareholder resolution at a European bank, calling on UK-based Barclays, as a big lender to fossil fuel companies, to bring its lending in line with the Paris Agreement and publish a plan to phase out such funding. 'It doesn't matter if you're not the biggest shareholder – you can still make your voice heard,' says Simon Webber, who manages a climate change fund at Schroders. Even professional fund managers are sometimes relative minnows as shareholders of larger companies, but they still try to engage. Schroders wrote to Amazon encouraging it to do more on electrification – and in 2019 the company announced that it would move to be net zero by 2040 and have a fleet of 100,000 electric vans.

The biggest investors are generally pension funds, sovereign wealth funds and university endowment funds: so-called asset owners, rather than asset managers. Like retail investors, they are looking for the best professionals to manage their money; unlike retail investors, they have so much money they can hire and fire those fund managers. The largest pension fund in the world, for example, the $1.5tn Government Pension Investment Fund of Japan, raised eyebrows in 2019 when it started shifting tens of millions' worth of assets to LGIM from one of LGIM's huge rivals, in a move that was widely interpreted as a lack of confidence in the rival's voting record on climate change at the companies it invested in. (The name of the rival has never been made public, but is an open secret in sustainable investing circles.)

Another active asset owner when it comes to climate change is the Church of England, which oversees £12bn in endowment and investment funds. In January 2020 it launched a passive index, the FTSE TPI Climate Transition Index, which it said was the first global index that allowed passive funds to back companies aligned to the Paris Agreement.

Using one's role as a shareholder to make demands is a position of power. Dr Quigley of Cambridge University says: 'I think a much more aggressive shareholder engagement needs to take hold where we fire directors if they're not aligned with the Paris Agreement.' She is also aware that an institution like Cambridge has clout with fund managers not because of its money – the endowment fund is 'only' worth £8bn – but because of its name.

Professional investors speaking up

Small investors can also work with big investors to effect change. The ShareAction resolution attracted attention from more than 10 institutional investors in Barclays as well. One of those, Sarasin & Partners, said: 'Given the systemic threats posed by climate change, and the rising regulatory scrutiny of banks' resilience to accelerated decarbonisation and climatic impacts, this resolution supports the long-term economic interest of shareholders.'

Professional fund managers who are overseeing hundreds of millions or billions of pooled money can have much greater clout with the company – and they are increasingly putting pressure on the companies they invest in to do more to combat climate change. Fund managers who use their clout to achieve change have traditionally been labelled activists – though that may have nothing to do with social responsibility. Some activist hedge fund managers are notorious for taking brutal action against companies they own purely to increase the share price value, which they would argue is their job. But now, with climate change so high on the agenda, a growing number of fund managers who wouldn't label themselves activists are speaking out. Some have banded together in groups.

At the end of 2017, many global fund management groups and other institutional investors, such as pension funds, signed up to the Climate Action 100+ initiative, which commits them to positively engaging with the companies they're invested in to get them to do more to combat climate change. The 100+ refers to the companies on its list: a combination of the world's 100 most polluting companies plus 61 others that are systemically important in some other way, for example by having a key role to play in the energy transition process.

A 2019 report from the group listed some of its achievements in the form of climate change promises that various of the 100+ companies had made as a result of investor engagement and pressure. These included Maersk, the world's biggest shipping company, committing to net zero emissions by 2050; Nestlé committing to net zero emissions by 2050; PetroChina developing a climate change strategy and signalling its intention to align its climate policy to the goals of the Paris Agreement; and Volkswagen committing to become climate neutral by 2050 and launching nearly 70 electric vehicle models by 2028. In May 2020, the group also claimed a victory after Total, the global energy company, followed recent steps taken by its peers BP and Shell to commit to zero emissions by 2050.

The Institutional Investors Group on Climate Change (IIGCC), a partner of the Climate Action 100+ group, is a collection of more than 230 European investors from 15 countries managing more than €30tn in assets. While it includes groups that are known for their history in environmental investing, such as Impax or Sarasin & Partners, it also contains some of the biggest fund managers across Europe, such as DWS in Germany, AXA in France and Goldman Sachs Asset Management. 'We're seeing institutional investors drive real change,' says Tom Fern, a spokesperson for the group.

Hoodwinking the fund managers too

When they're pushing for action on climate change at the companies they invest in, fund managers, just like retail investors, have to be alert to greenwashing. As we saw with Jenny's story, the worry with positive engagement is that companies are merely paying lip service to demands made by investors.

Certainly there is widespread awareness that it is a good thing to at least look concerned about the climate. This has led to some rather bizarre advertising campaigns. A Volvo video in January 2020, for example, followed a man who was attempting to save the Mauritius kestrel from extinction; the company's official Twitter account stated: 'Climate change is robbing the world of its biodiversity.' The connection with selling cars was not immediately evident. In October 2019, in fairness, Volvo had said it planned to reduce the carbon footprint of every car by 40 per cent between 2018 and 2025, as part of its plan to become carbon neutral by 2040.

Yet there are, in general, some issues around the emissions pledges that companies are starting to make. This can be a problem for professional investors trying to work out whether they should put a company in their climate-aware fund. Just as claims about green products are aimed at getting more consumers to buy them, claims about environmental credentials may be aimed at investors and banks in the hope of attracting more investment or funding. The easiest sector to be sceptical about here is, unsurprisingly, the oil and gas industry, where pledges to be more renewable are often taken with a pinch of salt by canny investors.

In April 2020, Royal Dutch Shell announced plans to slash its carbon output, becoming the biggest global energy group to introduce a net zero emissions target after a lengthy campaign from a group of its climate-conscious shareholders, including the Climate Action 100 + group. Yet some people were not convinced. Shortly after Shell's announcement, shareholder campaign group ShareAction recommended that shareholders reject the company's pay policy at its annual meeting in May, on the grounds that it would incentivise further extraction and burning of fossil fuels, 'activities which are clearly misaligned with the company's strategy to reach the goals of the Paris Agreement'.

Industrial group Ineos, which owns or sponsors various sporting groups including France's OGC Nice football club, has been accused by environmental activists of using sport to greenwash its image and divert attention from its environmental impact. A huge supplier of materials used in plastics, paint and medicines, Ineos operates a collection of refineries, offshore gas fields and chemical works, and has been criticised over its support of shale gas extraction via fracking in the UK.

In February 2020, Delta Airlines said it would offset all its carbon emissions by 2030, spending $1bn to increase fuel efficiency on flights as well as plant trees and build wetlands. Yet analysts at Morgan Stanley noted cynically that such announcements by airlines were evidence of their efforts to 'reduce government scrutiny over industry emissions'.

In 2019, BP launched a huge ad campaign called 'Possibilities Everywhere' with videos showing solar energy solutions, emphasising its commitment to energy alternatives. But in December that year, it faced legal action over the campaign after environmental lawyers from ClientEarth, a non-profit legal group, submitted an official complaint, arguing that BP was misleading consumers over its low-carbon credentials. Sophie Marjanac, a ClientEarth lawyer, told the *Financial Times*: 'BP is spending millions on an advertising campaign to give the impression that it's racing to renewables, that its gas is cleaner and that it is part of the climate solution. This is a smokescreen.'

Yet in February 2020, with a new chief executive recently installed, BP made a surprise announcement that it planned to achieve net zero emissions by 2050, in what was hailed as the most ambitious climate change commitment yet from one of the oil and gas industry's biggest companies. The *Financial Times* noted that BP had faced 'twin pressures' from shareholders: from those who wanted it to move more quickly towards clean energy and those who wanted to keep their juicy dividends. The company also announced it would ditch the much-criticised advertising campaign, basically accepting that it came across as hypocritical.

Improving disclosure

To avoid letting companies off the hook, professional and individual investors are increasingly using their positive engagement with companies on climate change to call for more specific targets that are harder to shirk. One of the first ports of call tends to simply be disclosure: there is currently no law requiring companies to disclose their carbon emissions, let alone requiring them to have a plan for how to reduce them.

In December 2019, hedge fund manager Christopher Hohn – whose fund is not specifically an environmental one – called on various companies including Airbus and Moody's to improve their pollution disclosure or he would vote against their directors. He told the *Financial Times*: 'Investing in a company that doesn't disclose its pollution is like investing in a company that doesn't disclose its balance sheet. If governments won't force disclosure, then investors can force it themselves.'

Each year, non-profit organisation the CDP (formerly the Carbon Disclosure Project) asks global companies and cities to measure and report what climate change means for their business. Not all respond, though there was an 11 per cent jump in respondents on the previous year for the most recent report, in 2018. At that time, more than half of responding companies were yet to set an absolute target for their emissions. Investors are also asking companies to put pressure on their suppliers to reduce their carbon emissions as well. These are so-called scope 3 emissions, which we'll discuss later in the book, and which can account for the majority of a company's total emissions.

In addition to simply disclosing their emissions, investors are also pushing companies to do more to disclose the risks to their business from climate change. There is currently no official way of measuring this, so there is an element of subjectivity, and possibly obfuscation, to the process. The CDP report found that less than half of the companies with headquarters in the US, Brazil, Mexico, Thailand, Argentina and Chile reported risks that could have a substantive impact. But at the other end of the spectrum, at least three quarters of those based in Turkey, the Republic of Korea, Indonesia, New Zealand and South Africa said they thought there were substantive risks to their business from climate change. As climate change doesn't tend to differ too much between countries, this discrepancy could have more to do with the local politics and/or measuring standards of each country rather than the actual risk level.

Banks are another key target of climate-conscious

investors. Many of the world's leading financial institutions are coming under increasing pressure to lend less, or not at all, to polluting companies or for polluting projects. In February 2020, J. P. Morgan, which has faced pressure from activists who accuse it of being the world's biggest banker of fossil fuels, said it was banning new lending to oil and gas development in the Arctic and imposing new limits on financing coal businesses. The move did not go down well in all circles, with climate action group 350.org calling on the bank to stop lending to fossil fuel companies altogether and divesting from coal companies in its asset management business. The *Washington Post* called the move a 'baby step'. But it was a step. And a similar move in December 2019 by Goldman Sachs, which became the first US bank to establish a 'no-go' zone in the oil and gas sector by ruling out direct financing for Arctic exploration, was praised by environmental groups.

Some banks, rather than divesting their financing, are engaging with companies, just like shareholders do, to try and help them improve their environmental credentials. In 2017, Dutch health technology company Philips took a €1bn loan from lender ING, along with other banks, whose interest rate depended on the company's ability to improve its sustainability rating. The better its ESG score, as measured by independent company Sustainalytics, the lower its debt payments would be. That's a bit like your mortgage payments going down if you recycle more. France's Danone did something similar in 2018, and in the US, CSM Energy also accepted what has been dubbed a 'sustainability-linked loan'.

Investors and shareholder action groups have successfully lobbied for other specific resolutions at companies. Following engagement with US shareholder action group As You Sow, the Kellogg Company said in January 2020 that it would phase out the use of glyphosate, the world's most widely used weedkiller, linked to health issues in humans as well as bees. In 2018, Thai cement company Siam Cement set carbon emissions reduction targets for 2023 and 2030 following engagement with one of its shareholders, Hermes, which is widely seen as one of the most active fund managers on positive engagement over sustainability issues, with a history of engagement and results at companies from BP to Anglo American.

The world needs innovation to combat climate change, and we'll look at companies with great ideas in the following chapters. But existing companies transitioning to a low-carbon era is also a big theme. Investors can help companies to do this by rewarding them for their efforts: buying their shares when they disclose climate-friendly targets, or helping to finance environmentally friendly projects through green bonds those companies issue.

In the energy sector, which we'll look at in more detail in Chapter 5, we'll see that oil and gas companies need to transition to alternative energy sources. If shareholders like those involved with the Climate Action 100+ initiative put pressure on them, that could help to speed up the energy transition. Some people argue that it could even be damaging, at this early stage of the energy transition, to dump fossil fuel stocks altogether. A January 2020 report by Bank of America Merrill Lynch warned that as energy companies had already been a frequent target of divestments, a key risk for the energy transition was that there wouldn't be enough capital investment in the sector in the years ahead to sufficiently support a seamless transition to a low-carbon economy.

Identifying and measuring risks is seen as crucial for investors in a climate change era, as it will help them to understand how different companies are adapting to climate change and who the winners and losers will be. There is still a lot of work to be done in this area, including calls for central banks and regulators to be more involved; we will return to this topic in the conclusion.

How to be an activist

How can retail investors get involved in positive engagement? One way is to do what Jenny did: buy shares in companies, join shareholder action groups, go to AGMs and write to the directors of companies you own.

But it's not always necessary to buy direct shares in a company. Buying individual shares exposes investors to more risk – and as we saw in Chapter 2, retail investors are generally advised to spread their risk. Many investors will find themselves buying funds instead. The most obvious place to look is at climate change or environmental funds, where the fund managers will hopefully be putting pressure on companies to change themselves, as in the examples we discussed above.

Business in these funds has been booming: we've seen that in 2019, investors ploughed a record $20.6bn into US sustainable investment funds, almost four times as much as the previous year. We'll look more in the following chapters at some of the specific opportunities these funds can offer across sectors like energy, transport and agriculture. Remember, though, that even among sustainable investment funds, there can be big differences in approach. Such funds all work in different ways – some have a negative screening process, others only invest in companies mainly engaged in solving climate change, others are more or less activist.

We saw in the last chapter that Morningstar, for example, thinks that low-carbon or ex-fossil fuels make sense for those more interested in divestment. For many investors, however, the choice between ex-fossil fuel funds and climate solution funds may not be straightforward. Investors in low-carbon and ex-fossil fuel funds may be missing out on exposure to carbon solutions because oil and gas companies, as we will see in the next chapter, are increasingly developing products and services that address climate change. 'The companies that pollute the most are also the ones with the biggest financial muscle who are doing a lot of research and development and looking to provide solutions – it's not that black and white,' notes Hortense Bioy, a director of sustainable research at Morningstar.

Yet there is no need to choose between avoiding fossil fuels altogether and investing in funds that include them. Some investors may prefer to have a strategy of owning low-carbon funds, for example, as that would expose them to greater diversity across sectors while not holding the worst-polluting companies, as well as climate solution funds that are more at the cutting edge of new technologies and ways of solving climate change.

Climate change or environmental funds may also only hold companies that are doing the majority of their work in this area, so if you want to engage rather than divest, such funds might not include mainstream companies that are working to cut their carbon emissions. Investors who want to support companies doing this could start by looking for fund managers who are trying to engage more in general with the companies they own: those who are signed up to the Climate Action 100+, for example.

Yet investors will still have to make their own decisions here, and may not wish to invest in certain companies even when they are brandishing their environmental credentials. Take the RE100 initiative: a list of companies created by reputable climate change body the Climate Group in partnership with the CDP that are committed to using 100 per cent renewable energy in their operations. It includes various companies one would not associate with climate change as such, including J. P. Morgan Chase and Wells Fargo, the two banks identified as the biggest fossil fuel financiers in a 2019 report by the Rainforest Alliance Network. It also contains SGS, an inspection company that on the one hand can help fossil fuel companies to minimise their environmental footprint but on the other, according to its website, has a 'comprehensive range of services for the coal industry' – including those to do with exploration. Whether investors want to reward them by buying their stocks will be a personal choice.

Just as investors should be wary of companies that say they're doing good things on the environment but may just be paying lip service to a trend, they should also be wary of professional investors who say they're investing with climate change in mind. One test of how committed an institutional investor is to pushing for change at a company is to examine their voting records when it comes to climate-related resolutions – much as one can examine the voting record of one's local politician on certain issues. Climate-related resolutions are usually discussed at AGMs held by listed companies and can range from requiring companies to simply disclose their emissions to setting emissions targets.

You could do this, for example, by looking up a 2019 report by ShareAction, which analysed the voting records of some of the world's biggest institutional investors on climate-related resolutions. The results did not point to a great appetite for change among the management of the companies themselves: of the 65 resolutions analysed, the management and boards rejected the resolutions and recommended shareholders vote against them in all but one case. The report also found that US institutional investors tended to vote far less than their European counterparts in favour of climate-related resolutions: those voting in favour less than 10 per cent of the time included Capital Group, BlackRock, T. Rowe Price, J. P. Morgan and Vanguard. Those most likely to vote in favour were led by UBS at 90 per cent, followed by Allianz Global Investors, Aviva Investors, HSBC Asset Management, LGIM and AXA Investment Managers.

Rather surprisingly, 6 out of 10 of the worst performers in terms of their voting record on climate change resolutions were also supporters of the Taskforce for Climate-Related Financial Disclosures (TCFD), which is pushing for companies to disclose their carbon emissions, suggesting an alarming degree of greenwashing. Many of the resolutions that they voted against were modest, too: most simply called for companies to disclose more about their exposure to risk, rather than for any concrete action. This lack of action by some institutional investors has led to criticism. In January 2020, a coalition of shareholders including nuns, public pension funds and asset managers filed resolutions at BlackRock, Vanguard, J. P. Morgan and T. Rowe Price calling for the fund houses to review their voting policies on climate change issues.

A separate ShareAction report in 2018 looked at the voting records of some of the UK's largest professional investors with environmental, social and governance mandates from charitable clients and found that many were voting with the company even when most other investors voted against. One ShareAction spokesperson told the *Financial Times* that 'too few asset managers are willing to upset cosy relationships'.

BlackRock, as the largest investment manager in the world, with $7tn of assets, has particular clout. Yet it was the company cited time and time again by people interviewed for this book as the biggest culprit of greenwashing. One of the worst offenders in the Share-Action report, it has frequently faced heavy criticism for its failure to back climate resolutions at the companies its funds invest in. A separate report from Majority Action, a US-based shareholder action group, found that 16 climate-related resolutions would have been passed in 2019 if BlackRock and Vanguard had voted for them, with the two between them often holding at least 10 per cent of the shares of the companies where the resolutions were filed. These would have included making engineering company Fluor set emissions reduction targets, forcing ExxonMobil to report on its lobbying activities and compelling various other energy companies to disclose their expenditure on political activities. Christopher Hohn, the hedge fund manager who wanted companies to disclose more about their polluting activities, has also publicly criticised BlackRock for its poor record on climate change resolution votes.

In January 2020, however, BlackRock promised it would hold companies to account on climate change, signing up to the TCFD and undertaking to put climate risk at the heart of its investment decisions. This was widely hailed as a good sign for those worried about climate change and a positive message to other investors – and BlackRock reiterated its promise as the coronavirus hit the global economy in March. It also took some bolder steps, such as criticising Siemens for its role in a controversial Australian coal-mining project, though activists were not satisfied. Greenpeace in Germany pointed out that BlackRock still backed the board of Siemens: 'This clearly exposes [BlackRock chief executive] Larry Fink's pledges to promote sustainability as blunt greenwashing,' it said in a statement.

In short, while the world's largest asset managers are starting to make the right noises on climate change and put more pressure on companies to cut carbon emissions, many of them still have a patchy record. Investors might prefer to put their money with fund houses that have consistently focused on the environment or engaged with companies properly on ESG issues. These include Impax Asset Management, which has run the Impax Environmental Markets fund since 2004; Sarasin & Partners, which manages money for charities as well as retail investors and has a history of pushing for change at companies it invests in; or Triodos Investment Management, another sustainable investment specialist.

Put pressure on your pension manager

For many investors, their pension will be their main investment. As we've seen, some workplace pensions will offer a sustainable option. However, a company's 'ethical' fund choice may not be what you had in mind, and it may not be focused on environmental issues. You can check whether it aligns with your expectations by looking at the fund factsheet. In the UK, for example, the government has set up a workplace pension scheme called Nest. One of the funds held in Nest's ethical option is the BMO Responsible Global Equity fund. Google this and go to the fund factsheet, or portfolio link, which will show you the fund's top 10 holdings (these are the only holdings that funds are required to disclose publicly). The top company, as of early 2020, was Microsoft, followed by Apple and Mastercard. These are not obviously ethical companies, or aligned with climate change awareness.

This doesn't necessarily mean that the fund is wrong, or unethical, or even being deliberately misleading. You may decide in some cases that the names funds give themselves *are* deliberately misleading: that greenwashing is taking place. But in many cases confusion stems from the mistaken, though understandable, belief that sustainable funds only hold companies whose main business is sustainability.

The top holding of the fund, Microsoft, was named by the CDP as among the leading companies in the world in terms of corporate climate action, even though it doesn't specifically create products or services to combat climate change. One of the BMO fund managers, Jamie Jenkins, told the *Financial Mail on Sunday* in 2019 that the reason it held Apple was because the company uses renewable energy across its business operations. Some investors may find this perfectly reasonable: it's an example of investing in 'best in class' companies that aren't obviously linked to climate change. Others may feel that a global technology company that has been criticised for constantly churning out new products and making it hard to repair old ones is not what they had in mind when investing to save the planet. A case can be made either way. 'Best in class' is one of the strategies that investors who prefer to engage rather than divest often use. It means investing in the company that is making the most effort in its sector to combat climate change (the concept also applies in the social and governance spheres). It can be seen as a way of rewarding the company; the fact that such a company may have environmentally minded shareholders is also a sign that it tends to engage with them and may have changed its practices for the better previously.

What can you do if your workplace pension doesn't offer you what you consider a decent ethical fund or climate change option? It is possible to press for change. Write letters to your company, and to the trustees of your pension. If enough people make a noise, pension providers will make an effort to offer more sustainable solutions – or your company might switch provider. Kate Brett, who heads up sustainable investing in the UK at Mercer, which consults pensions on their schemes, says that she's seeing increasing interest from pension trustees in adding ESG principles to the default pension fund. While she estimates this is happening in less than 5 per cent of company pensions currently, she says the situation is changing rapidly and she expects it to be 'considerably more' in a couple of years. In fact, in 2019, the UK pensions regulator said that 'Climate change is a core financial risk which trustees will need to consider when setting out their investment strategy.'

Some pension funds are laying a path for others to follow. The world's largest pension fund, the Government Pension Investment Fund of Japan, has a particular interest in sustainable issues, and Hiro Mizuno, the fund's chief investment officer, has said that failing to integrate ESG factors is contrary to the fiduciary duty of long-term professional investors.

Some people believe that regulators should be doing more, for example by requiring default funds to be invested with climate change in mind. 'You shouldn't be able to get a government-approved default pension in this country [the UK] unless it's Paris-aligned,' argues Jeremy Oppenheim, Systemiq founder. 'How can you possibly say it's safe to a 25-year-old if it's not giving a stable climate future?'

Invest in green bonds

Another way to influence a company is through its bonds, and as we've seen, a lot of voices in the climate change space argue that this is an increasingly effective route.

Retail investors don't buy single company bonds themselves, as the barrier to entry is too high. That means they're unlikely to be in a position to talk to company directors, as they might be by holding direct shares in a company. But they can indirectly show their support for companies by helping to finance green bonds, or transition bonds, through mutual bond funds.

The first green bond was issued by the European Investment Bank in 2007, and while green bonds have mostly been issued by companies since then, European countries including France, Poland, Belgium and Ireland have also been getting in on the act, with green government bonds available to investors since 2016. Institutional investors in the UK, including Threadneedle's Simon Bond, started calling on the government to issue green bonds in 2019, after it took the unusual step of declaring a climate change emergency in May that year.

According to Climate Bonds Initiative, a not-for-profit watchdog, green bonds had a record year of inflows in 2019, hitting $1tn in total as companies and governments around the world issued them. Yet that is still a small amount compared with conventional bonds. The green bond market is also much more highly concentrated in certain sectors. Remember the rule of thumb with investing that it is a good idea to spread your risk across different types of sector. Green bonds are most commonly issued by utility companies, banks and European companies, meaning that investors in green bonds face a somewhat restricted investment universe. By February 2020, more than three quarters of the green corporate bond market came from the US or Europe – which alone accounted for nearly 60 per cent, according to a report from Deutsche Bank. Utility companies made up 39 per cent of the total, while banks accounted for 33 per cent.

This lack of choice extends to bond funds for retail investors as well. 'If I had a wishlist,' says independent financial adviser Robin Keyte, 'it would be for the development of more ethical bond funds.' He has complained to fund managers about the lack of options, he says, but they reply that it is an issue of demand: if more people ask for them, they will launch new products.

Another new concept in the green bond space is transition bonds. These can be issued by 'brown' companies and usually create some sort of financial incentive for the company to clean up its act. There are currently only a handful of so-called transition bonds out there, but analysts predict this market will grow.

Improving the climate footprint of existing companies is a key strategy in helping to cut global emissions generally. Yo Takatsuki, head of ESG research at London-based AXA Investment Managers, told the *Financial Times* in January 2020: 'The 2010s was the decade we saw an awakening of the concept of green but the 2020s will be defined by the concept of transition.' And just as equity managers can put pressure on companies they invest in to set better carbon emission targets, bond investors can do the same. Wim Van Hyfte, head of ESG at European asset manager Candriam, says his firm has told at least one company they will not refinance their debt unless they set clear carbon emission targets.

Others are suspicious about the idea of a polluting

company issuing a supposedly green bond, fearing greenwashing in some cases. In October 2019, Teekay Shuttle Tankers, a Bermuda-based shipping company that transports oil from offshore drilling sites, attempted to raise money from investors for a 'green' bond that would finance the construction of fuel-efficient tankers. It failed to reach its target after some investors called the idea 'oxymoronic'. Ideally, a bond fund manager would be able to see through greenwashing cases, though you should always check yourself that you're happy with what a bond fund is investing in.

Explore passive investing

The debate between active and passive investing has been hotly contested this century. In recent years, the allure of so-called 'star' fund managers has faded amid various scandals. One noteworthy case is UK fund manager Neil Woodford's fall from grace. At one time the best-known fund manager in the country, he was forced to close his flagship fund in 2019 after investors rushed for the exit following a period of poor performance. This cult of personality around often underperforming active fund managers has only helped the case for passive funds, which have become ever more popular in recent years, especially in the United States. These funds are much cheaper, and retail investors will often buy exchange-traded funds that track a selection of global indices to make sure they are exposed to different countries and sectors. But where does this leave engaging with companies?

There are many passive ESG funds that investors can buy – the catchily named ESG ETFs (exchange-traded funds). The first was created back in 1990.[*] Modern ones are often adapted from a 'parent' index: the MSCI World, for example, is an index of the world's largest companies. The MSCI World ESG index will exclude some companies from the parent index and weight others differently. Moving all your ETF investments to their ESG counterparts would be one option.

From the point of view of professional passive fund managers, it is still possible to engage with the management of a company, says the UN's Principles for Responsible Investment body, which launched a consultation paper with the industry in 2019 on how best to achieve this. Indeed, as we've seen, the world's largest ETF providers, including Vanguard, BlackRock and State Street, have come under pressure to be more engaged. While active fund managers can express their displeasure with a company that doesn't take action on climate change by selling it, this is not an option for passive fund managers. Some people argue that that makes their voting power even more important, as they are always present, and are often significant shareholders. Yet because they have so many holdings across so many companies and don't have the time to vote themselves, research on how to vote is often 'outsourced' to third

---

* The even more catchily named MSCI KLD 400 Social Index.

parties such as proxy voting agencies. This has drawn criticism, as voting is deemed to be an important part of shareholder responsibilities.

However, passive investment is no longer seen as an excuse for ignoring climate change inaction. LGIM in the UK is, at the risk of sounding oxymoronic, one of the more active passive fund managers out there. It achieved something of a coup when it attracted tens of billions in 2019 from Japan's government pension fund, which was widely seen as approval of its tendency to engage more with the companies it holds. A spokesperson for LGIM says that while it can't divest holdings in passive funds, it can try to influence companies in other ways. For example, it can engage with index providers and make sure that there are robust standards to allow companies to list on the stock market in the first place. Some people have suggested that rules around disclosing carbon emissions should be made mandatory for companies wanting to list, for example.

Passive investors can also still ask companies to change. In 2019, for example, LGIM wrote to 19 Japanese companies that had no women on their boards and asked them to do more to promote women into senior roles, leading many to improve their gender diversity scores. And engaging leads to financial rewards for investors. Overall, LGIM says that if it engages with companies on an environmental, social or governance theme, the ESG scores tend to go up, and this tends to improve returns as well.

Will had considered himself a climate-conscious consumer for a while. He had already looked into personal ways of reducing emissions: going vegetarian, flying less, switching his energy provider to a greener alternative. Then he realised that another step would be to change the way his money was invested. He started by writing to his pension provider to ask them why they didn't consider environmental, social and governance principles when they were investing. He didn't have much luck at the time. But more recently, he says, he's noticed that, in line with the changing attitude of smaller savers and investors, the pension provider has started publishing an analysis of the impact of its investments on society. 'It's basically a hobby for me: trying to use my money to reduce the impact of the emissions that these companies make,' he says.

Will banked with Nutmeg, a digital wealth manager in the UK that launched in 2012 and prides itself on transparency, using technology as well as passive funds to keep costs low. In 2018, Nutmeg introduced what it called socially responsible investment portfolios, and Will was quick to put his money in. But then he thought he should find out what he was actually investing in. He asked Nutmeg if he could see the main holdings in the portfolio. 'BP made up about 1 per cent of it,' he says. 'I was like, these guys aren't socially responsible: you can't make this claim that they are.' Nutmeg wrote in a blog that it understood why 'it may seem counter-intuitive' for a socially responsible portfolio to hold positions in fossil fuel companies, but that it believed the best way to influence responsible behaviour was by investing in companies that were taking steps to improve their carbon footprint: an example of the 'best in class' approach we've discussed in this chapter. Still, it was not what Will had expected. He went further: did Nutmeg actually engage with the companies in its portfolios directly? Given that they were held through tracker funds operated by another bank, this seemed unlikely.

He decided to take the activist approach. 'I decided it was probably better keeping my money in there for the moment and trying to influence Nutmeg, which [he laughs] is completely the opposite of the way I think they should behave with companies like BP. Nutmeg probably don't come from a place that I'm coming from – they might have a fund doing their bit for the planet, but realistically it's not enough, and I don't know whether that's Nutmeg's fault; it's probably the fault of the financial system.'

When I investigated further to find out why Will had been confused, I discovered that Nutmeg's portfolios are mainly made up of exchange-traded funds: passive investments that track an index of companies. One of these mentioned on its website is the UBS MSCI United Kingdom IMI Socially Responsible UCITS ETF – a veritable nightmare of acronyms. Its holdings include BP, as well as mining company Rio Tinto. While UBS, the Swiss wealth manager, has put its name on the fund, it is MSCI, the index provider, that created it and decided what companies should be in it. The UK fund that Will held is one of a family of MSCI global socially responsible indices, which MSCI says 'include companies with outstanding sustainability profiles, while excluding companies whose products' social or environmental impact is considered to be negative by values-based investors'.

Will doesn't believe that Nutmeg was greenwashing. Its socially responsible portfolios don't say that they won't invest in oil and gas companies (they do specifically say they will exclude tobacco companies and nuclear weapons manufacturers, for example). But he and his investment provider were obviously not on exactly the same page when it came to an understanding of what socially responsible meant.

Will's experience highlights the confusion and inconsistency over fund labelling that exists in the financial industry. At its least harmful, retail investors are confused about what they're investing in. At its most, financial advisers and professional investors believe that some funds are taking advantage of the growing interest in climate change investing and ESG in general, and that mis-selling scandals are inevitable.

It is often hard to say who is responsible for investigating and disclosing information, given the complex chain of financial companies involved in getting a product to the end consumer. In Will's case, should Nutmeg have queried UBS, the ETF provider, more? Or should UBS have asked MSCI why BP was in its fund? Or should MSCI have been clearer about why it put BP in its socially responsible index in the first place? Probably all three. But in the absence of clear regulations or standards on clarity, nobody is at present doing anything wrong.

Different fund managers will also have varying definitions of what they believe qualifies as ESG or sustainable. While UBS was happy to rely on MSCI's calculation of what counts as ESG, others would not be. Triodos Investment Management, a sustainable specialist fund manager, has analysed ESG indices and considers that of the top 10 companies in many of them, only one or two are genuinely sustainable. Whether a company should be considered sustainable is an ongoing discussion, says Roeland Tso, an investment analyst at Triodos. He says that the firm is very targeted in its selection of global companies that it thinks are contributing to a world of lower carbon emissions: it has an investment universe of 250 companies, from a total potential of over 1,600 in the MSCI World Index. These include companies in transition as well as sustainable ones. It holds weekly discussions about whether those should be included – and sometimes these result in a decision to get out. For example, Triodos was a shareholder in Spain's Siemens Gamesa Renewable Energy until 2019, when it decided to sell the company due to concerns that it could be violating human rights in its business operations in the occupied territories of Western Sahara. However good its environmental contribution was, it failed on the S score of ESG: a frequent balancing act that fund managers face.

Listing companies as ESG has sometimes led to confusing marketing through no direct fault of the fund manager. Fidelity was embroiled in controversy in 2019 after a *Sunday Times* investigation based on a report from SCM Direct found that several funds listed on its website as ESG owned tobacco, oil and weapons companies. The problem seemed to be that Fidelity had been using third-party data from Morningstar to classify whether a company was ESG or not. The firm responded swiftly, thanking the report authors for bringing it to their attention.

One reason for the confusing issues that can arise is that there are currently no set standards for how to measure climate change risk or define sustainability, though the European Union has been working on what it calls a green taxonomy. Ratings providers also have different standards for measuring how ethical or environmental a company is.

Index provider MSCI, for example, ranked Tesla as one of the best car manufacturers for ESG credentials, as it had a system that weighted its superiority on the environmental level. Yet FTSE rated it as one of the worst, as its system paid more attention to the governance level.

Two other ratings providers, Sustainalytics and Bloomberg, only agree on similar ratings for the same company two thirds of the time. That is relevant, as the ESG score of a company will often determine whether a fund manager will include it in their ESG fund.

Remy Briand, head of ESG at MSCI, says that the question of what a retail investor expects from their ESG fund is one they get a lot, but says: 'We're trying as much as we can to bring transparency to the methodology.' In May 2020, MSCI published more information on the characteristics of its ESG indices. Briand argues that the belief that ESG equals divestment is 'the most fundamental misunderstanding that's important to address'. Will's experience of discovering that he held BP in an ESG fund, then, may have been less an issue of greenwashing and more an issue of this disconnect between how the retail investor and the industry understand financial labelling of sustainable products.

What can you do?

- If you have direct holdings in a listed company, write to the board members and outline your concerns. If you can, attend the AGM and ask questions.
- Join a group like ShareAction in the UK or As You Sow in the US to learn about the issues they are targeting.

- Don't be afraid to challenge funds you're thinking about investing in. Write to your pension fund or investment provider and ask them to explain their thinking, if it's not clear. This will force them to consider how they communicate and how they make decisions about what companies to include in their portfolios. And if they're not members of the Climate Action 100+ group, ask them why. Ask them what their record is on pushing for disclosure of carbon emissions at the companies they invest in, and encourage them to engage.
- Look at specific environmental or climate-themed funds. Consider whether the companies the fund holds match your expectation based on the name of the fund. Often they may not. Always check the top 10 holdings, which can be accessed by finding the fund factsheet – your financial adviser can find this for you, or it should be available on the fund manager website or a fund research platform like Morningstar.
- Investigate your company pension scheme and see if there is an ethical fund you could switch your money to. Remember to look at what that ethical fund is actually invested in and whether it feels right for you. If it doesn't look right, write to your company and your pension provider. Ask them to make better options available.

- Don't just search for funds based on their name. As we've seen, names can be misleading, but equally, some funds classified as low-carbon or ex-fossil fuel don't even reflect this in their name.
- Think about what you're willing to compromise on. Would you invest in a company with a really great idea to solve climate change if it treated its employees badly? Be aware of these contradictions: not all environmental companies or funds are completely ethical.

5

Clean Power: Investing in Energy

In 2013, Michael Bruun, a banker at Goldman Sachs, came across an interesting-looking opportunity in the energy market. Dong Energy, Denmark's biggest utility company, was struggling. Its profits had plunged the previous year, and it needed more cash to prop up its fledgling business in offshore wind. Bruun decided that Goldman should step in. His team invested $1.2bn in the company in return for a 19 per cent stake. The majority owner remained the Danish government.

When Goldman became a major shareholder, most of Dong's profits were coming from oil and gas. But Bruun believed that offshore wind could be much more profitable over time. For a company whose name was an acronym of 'Danish Oil and Gas', it was slightly awkward to have to explain to the company directors that it was actually not very good at doing oil and gas and that it would never compete that well with the global oil majors like BP or Shell. Bruun persuaded the new chief executive, Henrik Poulsen, whom he trusted and had done business with previously, to switch course and focus on offshore wind. Goldman had also inserted a clever clause when it made its initial offer for the company, meaning that its investment was dependent on Dong listing on the stock market: the main way for investors in a private company to make a whole lot of money at once. If it hadn't listed by mid 2018, the paperwork stipulated, then Goldman was allowed to sell its stake back to the government.

It never had to use that clause. In 2016, Dong Energy listed on the stock market and made its investors billions. Goldman sold the last of its stake in 2017 at a huge profit. By early 2020, Dong's shares were soaring, having risen more than 70 per cent since the start of 2019 to value the company at $46bn – almost 40 per cent of BP's size. A February article in the *Financial Times* said that the company, which had rebranded as Orsted, had 'become a magnet' for fund managers as climate change rose up the political agenda and investors searched for less polluting options in energy. Poulsen proudly announced that Orsted's long-term goal was to become the world's first green energy supermajor.

Energy is the grandfather of carbon dioxide emissions. In 2018, three quarters of the world's energy supply still consisted of fossil fuels, with oil making up 29 per cent, coal 25 per cent, renewables and nuclear 24 per cent and natural gas 21 per cent.* The terms 'CO$_2$ emissions' and 'greenhouse gas emissions' are often used interchangeably when talking about climate change: in fact, CO$_2$ is just one of the greenhouse gases (GHG), though it is the main one, accounting for 72 per cent of overall GHG emissions. Methane – where cattle and natural gas production are the main culprits – accounts for 19 per cent; nitrous oxide (cattle again and synthetic fertilisers) 6 per cent and so-called F gases 3 per cent.

Of that 72 per cent figure, fossil fuels are the main culprit. Combusting coal, oil and natural gas accounts for 88 per cent of global carbon dioxide emissions, with respective shares of 39 per cent, 31 per cent and 18 per cent, according to a 2019 report from the PBL Netherlands Environmental Assessment Agency.

The United Nations has warned that global emissions need to be cut by 7.6 per cent every year of this decade if we are to meet the 1.5 degrees Paris goal. Until 2020, emissions were growing at an average 0.9 per cent a year over the previous decade. Total greenhouse gas emissions, including from land-use change, reached a record high of 55.3 gigatonnes in 2018. To meet the 2 degrees goal, that figure needs to fall by 15 gigatonnes by 2030. To meet the 1.5 degrees goal, it needs to fall by 32 gigatonnes. To put that in context, while emissions fell considerably in the first few months of 2020 due to the coronavirus lock-

---

* The fact that these figures do not add up to 100 percent is due to rounding in the calculations.

downs, scientists predicted that the annual drop in global emissions would be just 7 per cent. So even though much of the global economy was shut down, it still wasn't enough to cut emissions by the required amount. That is why wider long-term structural changes are so important – and none more so than in energy.

The case for energy when it comes to investing to save the planet is all about the energy transition. Existing energy companies need to transition from relying on oil and gas to renewable sources or they may not survive. New technologies need to be developed, while existing technologies – such as solar and wind – need to scale up even more than they have done already. Existing energy companies will need to develop their own technologies through research and development or snap up innovative new companies. Irena, the international renewable energy association, says that renewable energy and energy-efficiency measures can potentially achieve 90 per cent of the required carbon reductions.

Transitioning away from oil and gas

Let's deal first with the issue of existing companies in transition, a huge theme across sectors, as we've seen already. The world has shifted its energy use on a large scale before. Energy transition is not a new concept. In the nineteenth century, the world shifted from biomass and wood to coal, while the twentieth century saw a shift to oil. Coal's market share rose from 5 per cent to 60 per cent between 1830 and 1914, peaking in the year the First World War broke out. Oil's market share rose from 1 per cent to 40 per cent between 1900 and 1973, peaking in the year of the first OPEC oil shock. Gas rose from 4 per cent in 1945 to 24 per cent today, according to a 2018 report from the Oxford Institute for Energy Studies.

The report concluded that the global energy industry was verging on its next energy transition, with wind and solar likely to be the fuel of the twenty-first century. The transition could be at a much faster pace, due to the pressure of regulation, in contrast to previous transition periods, which were more opportunistic. But historical examples have both fast and slow energy transition periods, making the pace this time around a critical uncertainty.

Still, everyone recognises that if we are going to meet the Paris commitments, the world now has to undergo its third energy transition: from coal, oil and gas to renewable energy. The challenge is how to achieve this quickly enough. The latest annual report on world energy from BP found that in 2018, primary energy consumption grew at a rate of 2.9 per cent, almost double its 10-year average of 1.5 per cent per year, and the fastest rate since 2010. Carbon emissions grew by 2 per cent, the fastest growth for seven years. Yet just a year later, there were signs of hope. Figures from the International Energy Agency (IEA) showed that global carbon emissions from energy were flat, at 33 gigatonnes, in 2019, a year when the world economy grew by nearly 3 per cent. This prompted hopes that energy emissions might have peaked. The head of the IEA, Fatih Birol, told the *Financial Times* in February 2020: 'The clean energy transition is starting to accelerate very strongly. This makes me hopeful we are seeing a peak in emissions and they will now start to decline.' He was speaking before the pandemic had hit. By April, the IEA predicted that global energy-related CO_2 emissions would fall by nearly 8 per cent in 2020, reaching their lowest level since 2010.

'No oil and gas company will be unaffected by clean energy transitions, so every part of the industry needs to consider how to respond,' the IEA said in its 2020 report. In April, noting the huge impact on oil demand of the global lockdowns, it said: 'It is still too early to determine the longer-term impacts, but the energy industry that emerges from this crisis will be significantly different from the one that came before.' What will not change, however, is the need for the energy transition. Dr Birol wrote in March that 'We should not allow today's crisis to compromise our efforts to tackle the world's inescapable challenge.'

Some companies were already transitioning, under pressure from regulators and governments. In 2015, the UK said it would shut down all coal plants by 2025, which helped the country's reliance on coal for electricity to fall from 70 per cent in 1990 to less than 3 per cent by 2020. That pushed companies to make real changes. Drax, the FTSE 250-listed UK power company, had already drastically reduced its reliance on coal and shifted to biomass, before announcing in February 2020 that it would stop using coal altogether in 2022, ahead of the deadline.

Yet investment by Big Oil in alternative energy sources has so far been underwhelming, to put it mildly. As of the start of 2020, investment by oil and gas companies outside their core business areas was less than 1 per cent of total capital expenditure, according to the IEA. Some were moving into new areas by buying existing companies, for example in the fields of electricity distribution, electric vehicle charging and batteries, while stepping up research and development activity. But the IEA said that a 'much more significant change' in how these companies allocated their cash would be required to accelerate energy transitions.

The transformation of the energy sector can happen without the oil and gas industry, the IEA argues, but it would be more difficult and more expensive, as these companies, with their huge existing infrastructure and cash piles, are in a good position to help accelerate and scale up new technologies. In particular, the IEA has called for companies to step up investment in low-carbon hydrogen, biomethane and advanced biofuels. By 2030, it says, these low-carbon fuels should account for 15 per cent of overall investment in fuel supply.

A bad taste in the mouth for clean energy investors

Some investors may be nervous about the idea of investing in renewable energy. They may remember the boom and bust of the 2000s, when investors piled into solar and wind energy but many companies went bust. BP somewhat infamously rebranded itself as 'Beyond Petroleum' as far back as 2001, proceeding to invest in solar and wind before quietly dropping the moniker after it shut down its solar business in 2011, claiming at the time that it was not profitable.

One major reason for the failed renewable energy push of the noughties was that renewable energy costs were not then competitive with mainstream energy costs. Companies therefore relied on government subsidies. That proved to be an unstable source, with the global financial crisis of 2008 leading some governments – notably in Spain, which had been a huge champion of solar energy – to slash subsidies. Meanwhile companies in the US and Europe went out of business after China introduced its own aggressive subsidies, which, combined with cheaper labour and production costs, helped to flood the market with supply when demand was still low, causing prices to crash.

In a now-infamous 2007 TED talk, John Doerr, a partner at Silicon Valley venture capital firm Kleiner Perkins, said: 'Green technologies – "going green" – is bigger than the Internet. It could be the biggest economic opportunity of the twenty-first century.' Unfortunately, good ideas do not always equal good investments. A 2016 report from MIT found that venture capital firms spent over $25bn funding clean energy technology start-ups between 2006 and 2011 and lost over half their money. As a result, it warned, funding had dried up in the cleantech sector.

A new dawn for cleantech?

Energy investors claim it is different this time. For one thing, renewable energy costs have come down substantially and are now comparable to mainstream energy. Even in 2013, US wind and solar costs were not commercial without subsidies. By 2018, they had more than halved. The Oxford Institute for Energy Studies argues that this cost deflation was 'nothing short of revolutionary for the global energy industry', stating: 'As a result, on a plant-level basis and excluding the cost of dealing with intermittency, wind and solar have emerged as very competitive sources of energy globally.' And the IEA noted in April 2020 that the only energy source that was set to grow in 2020 was renewables, thanks in part to their low operating costs.

The eagerness of Big Oil to diversify into renewable and alternative energy sources is good news for start-ups building new technology in this next wave of climate change investment, as the oil companies constitute a potential pool of buyers. The goal for most start-ups is either to list on the stock market or get bought by another listed or private company, making lots of money for the founders and early investors in the process. There are plenty of examples of this in the clean energy space. In February 2019, Shell bought Sonnen, a German rival to Tesla and Samsung in providing homeowners with lithium-ion battery packs powered by solar energy. The company had been founded by serial entrepreneur

Christoph Ostermann in 2010 and enabled users of its battery to cut monthly bills and rely on clean energy for most of their power needs. Those needing extra energy could connect to the power grid, while those with energy to spare could sell it to peers. In a sign of how rapidly developing technology can cut costs, the price of one of its batteries had fallen from €25,000 when it launched to just €5,000 by 2016.

After pulling out of solar power in 2009, Shell returned to it in January 2019 when it bought a 44 per cent stake in Nashville-based solar developer Silicon Ranch. Just the previous month, its rival BP had also re-entered the solar market for the first time since 2011 by taking a $200m stake in Europe's biggest solar developer, Lightsource Renewable Energy.

A November 2019 report in *Science Direct* analysed the renewable energy commitments of the top eight oil majors globally and made the perhaps unsurprising finding that those with larger existing oil reserves – Chevron, Petrobras and ExxonMobil – were less likely to have significant investments in renewables. The exception was BP, which has higher oil reserves than many of its peers but has done more in renewables. And the report has already been overtaken by events: BP announced in February 2020 under its new chief executive Bernard Looney that it would cut its carbon emissions to net zero by 2050, in what was the most ambitious climate target to date from a major oil company.

Big Oil is made up of seven supermajors – the world's largest publicly traded oil and gas companies: BP, Chevron, ConocoPhillips, Eni, ExxonMobil, Royal Dutch Shell and Total. Yet between them these companies only account for an estimated 10 per cent of emissions from industry operations and 15 per cent of production, according to the IEA. The majority of production is in the hands of state-owned oil companies. Writing in the *Financial Times* in March 2020, Nick Butler, chair of the Policy Institute at King's College London, noted drily: 'Their priority is to maximise revenue from the development of national resources. They are immune to divestment campaigns, regulations requiring them to explain the risks to their asset valuations resulting from climate policies, and theatre companies or art galleries that refuse to accept their sponsorship.' A more fruitful path, he argues, is to change consumer energy consumption by investing in new low-carbon technologies that will help shift consumer behaviour – things like LED lighting, smart energy meters in the home, or ways of storing solar energy off grid.

Many oil and gas companies are putting their hopes into carbon capture, use and storage (CCUS) technologies, where carbon emissions are captured then stored underground, potentially indefinitely. The IEA has called on governments to help support innovation in this field, as it estimates that it could support 7 per cent of the emissions savings required to comply with the Paris Agreement. Yet it is an area in need of development: the IEA estimates, for example, that 2,000 CCUS facilities will be needed by 2040, but as of 2019, only 19 existed.

Billy Parish didn't start out intending to run an energy company. Originally a student activist, he dropped out of Yale in 2002 to found the Energy Action Coalition, a youth-focused grassroots climate change movement later renamed the Power Shift Network. It was an easy decision, he says. 'I became consumed with the movement.' Parish set up California-based Mosaic in 2010 after spending years as a climate activist. 'I moved into the business side because I felt like we weren't going to win through altruism. A lot of people are still economically motivated and need to see the solutions: how do we catalyse and grow the clean energy economy so people can see it as a viable alternative?'

Rather than selling or renting solar panels, Mosaic offers solar loans to homeowners so they can install panels and use the savings from their electricity bills to pay back the interest, saving money over time.

Mosaic started out as a crowdfunded initiative to help people to invest in clean energy in their local communities. It raised over $20m from 5,000 individuals this way. 'We were the first to crack the nut for allowing non-accredited investors, not just rich people, to invest in clean energy in their communities,' Parish says. The first individual investor, though, was an unusual one: the singer Prince put up $250,000 of his own money that Parish then got others to match to create crowd-funded zero-interest loans to fund five projects. US regulation was a barrier to scaling the crowd-funding model on a national level, so he turned to traditional institutional investors as the company expanded.

Mosaic is now the leading lender for residential solar in the US, making over $3.5bn of loans in 2019 to 125,000 households. In fact, it created a new market in residential solar loans, which can be sold on to investors such as Goldman Sachs, other asset managers and insurance companies. It is still a private company, but its exit path is unclear, says Parish, with listing just one option, though it was profitable in 2018. One of its peers, SolarCity, was bought by Elon Musk's Tesla in 2016 for $2.6bn.

Parish says that the early individual investors in his company were crucial for its initial success, and wishes that wealthier investors would do more to invest with climate change in mind. 'We wouldn't be around if individuals hadn't used some of their private wealth to back us. There is a gigantic amount of private wealth out there: the worst example is foundations sitting on huge amounts of private capital and investing it in very traditional ways, which makes me absolutely crazy. The same is true for private families. I'm of the belief that we need millions of new clean energy businesses and a lot of those small businesses are funded by friends and family so we need them to step up.'

Clean energy solutions

Energy is an area where innovation and new technology are still needed. This is where environmentally minded billionaires can play a role. In fact, the world's richest man, Bill Gates, is now also one of the biggest investors in climate change. In 2015 he and a number of other billionaires set up a fund, Breakthrough Energy Ventures (BEV), to invest in new technologies connected to climate change. The group identified five main areas in need of investment – agriculture, buildings, electricity, manufacturing and transportation – and have so far committed $1bn to the fund between them.

Some of the things BEV is looking at include new technologies that can bring down the cost of solar and wind power even further to help it scale up and be stored more effectively; transmission technologies like high-voltage direct current (HVDC), which can transfer wind and solar power from where it is created to where it is needed; and smart, flexible power grid technology that can update old creaking systems based on electricity flowing only one way to passive consumers, to a new world where electricity is intermittent and local producers of electricity can send it back to the grid. The companies in the group's portfolio include Massachusetts-based Malta, which converts electricity from the grid into heat, stores it in molten salt, then converts it back to electricity and returns it to the grid when needed. Another company, Quidnet Energy, uses wells to store energy as pumped hydro, avoiding the need for mountains or lakes.

Cleantech investment highlights some ways in which investing in climate change solutions can be different to traditional investments. Recognising that cleantech can take a long time to develop successfully, the Breakthrough Energy fund has a time horizon of 20 years when it makes an initial investment. This makes it different from other early-stage investors. Normally venture capital or private equity investors expect to get a return on their investment – usually through the sale of the private company or when it lists on the stock market – within 10 years. Part of BEV's strategy is to give cleantech companies more time than normal investors would. A typical tech investor in Silicon Valley investing in a new, unproven technology might give the company a little money and a little time, and see how it does. That might be half a million dollars over six months. With cleantech, says Eric Toone at BEV, it needs to be more like $30m over five years. Unproven technology is a huge risk. There will be winners, but there will also be losers, and there is no way of telling for sure at the start. 'Nobody wants to be the first one into these things, everybody wants to know it's going to work,' he notes.

Interestingly, the 2016 MIT report argued that it wasn't necessarily the case that cleantech in the noughties was a bad investment as such, but that the wrong sort of investor was attracted to it – namely venture capitalists. One reason that it could be unsuitable for venture capitalists, according to the report, is that such investors have a typical time horizon of between three and five years to make their money back, and thus are impatient for technology to be developed and scaled up faster. The correct lesson from the failure of cleantech between 2006 and 2011 is that it 'clearly does not fit the risk, return, or time profiles of traditional venture capital investors. And as a result, the sector requires a more diverse set of actors and innovation models.' Breakthrough Energy, with its 'patient capital' approach, is one such model. Institutional investors like pension funds and sovereign wealth funds, which can wait for decades to make returns but are often inexperienced technology investors, are another source.

BEV is probably the most high-profile example of wealthy investors looking to fund start-up technologies in the energy space and beyond to help combat climate change. Clean energy is also a particular area of interest for family offices – investment funds set up and run by wealthy families with the sole purpose of investing their own money. Younger members of wealthy families tend to be particularly keen on environmental investments, and many are bridging the gap between the traditional philanthropy that wealthy families engage in and investing to achieve certain solutions. This is often in the form of impact investment – a term that has become very trendy in recent years in investment circles. Impact investments typically aim at some sort of social good – be it solutions to climate change, improving poverty, or female education. The impact achieved is supposed to be measurable, and investment returns may only be paid out if certain goals are met. Some impact investors are willing to potentially lose all their money, others are happy to receive a return below what they'd get elsewhere, while others aim to get just as good a return as they would in a normal investment. The energy transition and cleantech has attracted various impact investors, many of whom are individuals representing their families or family offices.

Nicole Systrom (who also happens to be married to the founder of Instagram, Kevin Systrom) is an adviser at Prime Coalition, a consultancy in Boston that tries to get philanthropists involved in backing market-based solutions to climate change. One of its early projects was Quidnet, which went on to get backing from Breakthrough Energy Ventures. But it might not have got that far had a group of philanthropists not funded it with an initial $1m to see if its technology would even work, Systrom says. At the time, it had modelled its technology but not done any field tests – meaning that traditional venture capitalists were too wary of the risks of failure.

So philanthropists had to be essentially prepared to lose their money: a climate change investment gamble. It worked, and the rest was history. Echoing Breakthrough's view on the matter, Systrom says: 'A lot of tech in this space is really risky and you need a different kind of investor than a 5–10-year closed-end venture investor. It matches well with the attributes of philanthropy: very risk-tolerant, very long time frame for a return, if there even is one.'

How to invest in clean energy

The Breakthrough Energy Ventures approach, while inspiring, is a niche form of investment available to the select few: those who can afford to tie up huge sums of capital and risk losing much of it over the next 20 years or more. Billionaires, in short. The model can't really be replicated by everyday investors, who are more likely to find themselves choosing more traditional private equity or venture capital funds, if they can afford the risk; or funds that invest in already-listed companies, where the returns won't be astronomical but the risks are considerably less.

Investors who want a low-cost way of accessing clean energy can check out various exchange-traded funds. Some of the largest clean energy funds in the world are those that track an index, according to figures from Morningstar. These include the iShares Global Clean Energy ETF, which tracks the S&P Global Clean Energy index, invested in wind energy companies Vestas and

SolarEdge Technologies; the Invesco Solar ETF or the Lyxor New Energy ETF.

One of the largest actively managed clean energy funds is the Pictet Clean Energy fund, whose manager, Christian Roessing, invests in three categories of company: renewables, electrification in transport, and smart or energy-efficient manufacturing. In fact, investors often put clean energy and transport in the same category, as transport is fuelled by energy, and green transport, as we'll see in the next chapter, is another area of huge interest.

We've seen that Morningstar reckons climate solutions or clean energy funds will suit investors looking to take advantage of the opportunities created by the transition to a low-carbon economy. Some of the companies held in such funds focus on renewable energy, like Siemens Gamesa Renewable Energy and Vestas. But many of the companies held in such funds may actually be in transition, with legacy business in polluting areas. SSE is a popular holding, for example: it develops and operates renewable energy across the UK and Ireland but also generates over two thirds of its electricity from gas, oil and coal. Even Orsted, the darling of renewable energy investors that we discussed at the start of this chapter, and the world's largest renewable energy company, still has an energy mix consisting of 19 per cent coal and 17 per cent gas.

Funds in the area of climate solutions or clean energy or technology tend to be more suitable for investors with a high-risk appetite, as they often include smaller companies. They also have a narrower exposure, being more focused on tech or energy than, say, low-carbon funds that can invest in companies making efforts to reduce their carbon footprint across any industry or sector.

What can you do?

- Low-risk investors: you may want to consider investing in oil and gas companies that are setting zero emissions targets and doing research and development into renewable energy. These are likely to be very liquid and – for now – are still paying decent dividends. If this doesn't feel right for you, you could opt for low-carbon funds that own more pure-play renewable energy funds.
- Medium-risk investors: clean energy funds are often focused on new technology and can be riskier, but they offer a chance of getting involved in climate change solutions in a more direct way than low-carbon options. Climate solutions funds will also include newer companies that have invented new technology.
- High-risk investors: you probably won't be able to join Breakthrough with Bill Gates and the other billionaires, but if you have the money you could consider getting involved in energy start-ups that might be sold to the big oil and gas companies.

6

The Green Light:
Investing in Transport

In 2011, Horace Luke attended a small dinner party in Taipei. Over the main course, his host made him an unexpected offer of $50 million. Why? Luke had come up with an idea for electric mopeds that would help address the problem of pollution in his home town and beyond. It helped that his host, Samuel Yin, happened to be one of the richest men in Taiwan.

Luke had started his career at Microsoft, then worked at HTC, a Taiwanese smartphone company that back in 2011 was the largest smartphone vendor in the US, before it was overtaken by Apple and other rivals. There he met Yin. 'He asked if I wanted to build smartphones the rest of my life. I replied that I didn't: I wanted to work on sustainable products in transportation,' Luke recalls. 'I promised that the next time I saw him I'd have a plan, so I went to Rome and created a PowerPoint presentation about how I wanted to work on lightweight mobility so people could travel in densely populated cities more efficiently.'

After the presentation at dinner, Yin said: 'How do we make this happen?' Luke said he thought he could get a prototype made with $10–$20m. But that wasn't good enough for Yin. He said he wanted to make a dream come true, not just a prototype. How much would that cost? Luke said $50m. It was a deal right then and there. 'He literally stuck his hand out over the table and said, "I don't do contracts; I want to support you."' Nervously Luke clarified that he had meant US dollars, not Taiwanese dollars, which would have been worth significantly less. But his host had understood.

Luke's company, Gogoro, was Taiwan's first so-called 'unicorn' company: a private start-up worth more than $1bn. The idea behind it was simple: as cities begin to combat climate change, commuting by car will become more difficult. Gogoro produced its own electric mopeds but also, crucially, the battery infrastructure to support them: people could swap their old battery for a fully charged one at various charging points around Taipei. The company now sees about 200,000 battery swaps a day.

This form of micromobility is hot. Global consultancy McKinsey said in a 2019 report that investors had put $5.7bn into micromobility start-ups since 2015, with more than 85 per cent targeting China. It reckons the market could be worth up to

$500bn in the US, China and the EU by 2030 –
though its success will depend in large part on cities
putting the infrastructure in place to make it easier
for the vehicles to get around.

The electrification of transport

The interest in micromobility is part of a wider shift
emerging in how people get from one place to another.
The electrification of transport is the main frontier in
the battle to reduce pollution that accounts for 15 per
cent of greenhouse gas emissions globally, according to
the Centre for Climate and Energy Solutions. For all
the concern about air travel that most eco-minded consumers have, aviation is far from the biggest culprit: road
vehicles, including cars, trucks, buses, two- and three-
wheelers, make up nearly three quarters of total transport
emissions, according to the International Energy
Agency. The European Union says that cars and vans
alone account for 15 per cent of carbon dioxide emissions in the bloc, with all road transport – including
trucks and buses – accounting for 21 per cent as of 2016.

There are a few key areas that are in need of development. One is vehicles themselves, with mainstream car
companies from BMW to Volkswagen rolling out electric vehicles (EVs) as quickly as they can in anticipation
of even stricter regulations on emissions. And more
people using electric vehicles will not just help to reduce
transport emissions. It could have major knock-on

effects for energy emissions too. In a 2019 report, Irena said that electric vehicles promised to be 'a game-changer' for the world's shift to sustainable energy, and particularly to renewable power generation. It predicted that, with all kinds of cars spending 95 per cent of their time parked, electric vehicles hooked up to the grid while charging could form their own sort of micro-grids, helping to feed in electricity to the wider network when needed.

Unlike in swathes of the energy sector, governments have already set clear targets for electric vehicles, which is helpful for investors when measuring the likely size of the market and future returns on investment. The UK government said in 2020 that there would be no new sales of cars with internal combustion engines from 2035. The European Union introduced strict new regulations in January 2020 that require car manufacturers to reduce the average emissions of their fleets to 95 grammes of carbon dioxide per kilometre over the next two years or face hefty fines. In 2018, average emissions were 120 grammes, so that is effectively a 20 per cent reduction.

Clear regulations from governments are helpful for investors as they allow them to assess risk more effect-ively: the threat of significant fines means it is easier to predict that there will be a substantial new market in, for example, electric vehicle technology. Electric vehicles accounted for more than 2.5 per cent of all car sales in 2018, the IEA says, meaning there is some considerable way to go on a global level.

The global leader is Norway, where 56 per cent of new vehicles bought in 2018 were electric – way ahead of the second in line, Iceland, at 24.5 per cent. Norway has long had subsidies for electric vehicles, and shifting its cars to use electricity is an obvious next step for the country, as its domestic energy is largely generated by hydropower, which is already a green electricity source. Sales of electric vehicles in the US, by contrast, accounted for under 2 per cent. The world's fleet of passenger road vehicles in 2018 was made up of 97.5 per cent internal combustion engines and 2.5 per cent electric, a report from Norwegian registrar and classification society DNV GL found. By 2050, it predicts, that will have transformed to 73 per cent electric and 27 per cent internal combustion.

But as with solar subsidies in the noughties, government support can lead to some volatility. Sales of electric vehicles were up 9 per cent around the world in 2019, with over 2.2m sold. Yet that 9 per cent growth rate was a lot lower than in previous years, thanks in large part to China's decision to cut subsidies. The country, which accounts for about half of global EV sales, has been under pressure to reduce handouts after state support helped hundreds of local start-ups to flourish and raised concerns about a bubble in the industry.

EV Volumes, which collates monthly figures on electric vehicle sales, warned that the coronavirus fall-out could further impact sales in 2020, though this was likely to apply to sales of all cars as factory production slowed. A report from Wood Mackenzie, an energy consultancy, in April 2020 warned that electric vehicle sales were likely to drop drastically for the year, predicting global sales of just 1.3m, down from 2.2m in 2019. 'Most new EV buyers are still first-time owners of the technology,' a Wood Mackenzie analyst, Ram Chandrasekaran, wrote in a research note. 'The uncertainty and fear created by the [coronavirus] outbreak have made consumers less inclined to adopt a new technology.' But he added that once the epidemic was contained in China, consumers were expected to 'flock back to car dealers and reaffirm their confidence in EVs'.

The longer-term uptake of electric vehicles is, pandemic wobbles aside, expected to accelerate rapidly. From fewer than 500,000 passenger vehicles in 2010 to 6m in 2018, Irena predicts the world will see 157m by 2030 and more than 1.1bn by 2050, if Paris Agreement commitments are met.

The poster child for electric vehicles is Elon Musk's Tesla, which experienced exponential growth in its share price before the coronavirus market crash in February 2020. In just two months, from November 2019, its share price doubled, pushing its valuation to over $100bn – more than the share value at that time of General Motors and Ford put together. And that was for a company which – despite the odd profitable quarter – has still never turned an annual profit. Tesla would seem to be an obvious choice for any investor interested in investing to save the planet. Yet many sustainable investment funds have shunned it. That's because, while it ticks the environmental box in the ESG label, some investors believe it doesn't tick the other two. An analysis by Bloomberg in 2018 found that, out of 1,200 ESG funds, just 86 held Tesla – and only 7 of those had it as a top 10 holding. Concerns cited by investors ranged from executive pay to the lack of publicly disclosed sustainability goals. Tesla is often cited by sustainable investors as an example of how it's not necessarily simple deciding to invest in companies that are helping to save the planet.

At the other end of the spectrum, mainstream car companies are massively ramping up their production of electric cars and plan to outsell Tesla in the coming years. The world's largest car maker, Volkswagen, is hoping to sell a million emission-free cars in the three years to 2023, which would eclipse Tesla's sales. That is not to say that big car companies are now green activists. Volkswagen's record on this is hardly stellar, following the discovery that it had installed software that made its vehicles' emissions appear lower when being tested. In general, large car companies still rely heavily on sales of particularly polluting SUVs, regularly attracting the ire of climate change campaigners. Volkswagen as a company is by itself responsible for 1 per cent of global carbon dioxide emissions. Recognising this contradiction, the company said in February 2020 that it was going to appoint a climate campaigner to 'aggressively' challenge its environmental policies, with its chief executive admitting that it was not rolling out electric vehicles quickly enough.

Some mainstream investors believe that, as in other

sectors, investing in 'best in class' companies is a reasonable strategy when it comes to cars. The Schroders Global Climate Change fund, for example, has BMW as one of its top holdings. Simon Webber, one of the fund's managers, explains that while electric car sales are currently a tiny fraction of BMW's overall sales, the company is, in his view, the only major global car manufacturer apart from Tesla that has positioned itself well to enable the electric transition. 'Tesla might be the exciting one but it won't solve the problem by itself, and we believe that if you can identify a leader in "best in class" technology that is much better than its peers, that is going to be incredibly valuable,' he argues.

Unlike oil and gas companies, car companies are somewhat better able to adapt their business model to a world with tighter controls on carbon emissions. Yet unlike wind and solar energy, electric cars aren't yet competitive on cost, so more research and development is needed to achieve this. A 2019 report from BNP Paribas estimated that electric vehicles are likely to remain more expensive for the end consumer until 2023–5. Insurance for electric vehicles is also currently more expensive on average than for a standard car. There are many areas when it comes to electric vehicles and greener transportation in general in need of innovation – and this is where investors come in.

Obvious Ventures is a venture capitalist firm based in San Francisco that is notable for having tech star power at the helm: its co-founder, Ev Williams, was a co-founder of social media platform Twitter as well as chief executive of online publishing platform Medium. The firm is not dissimilar to Breakthrough Energy Ventures in that it invests in early-stage companies that it believes have the potential to change the world. One of its investments is in Proterra, which makes and designs zero emission buses. Another of Proterra's investors is Al Gore and David Blood's Generation Investment Management. Obvious was also an early backer of Beyond Meat, owning 9 per cent of the company when it floated on the stock market in 2019, paying its original investors huge returns.

Gabe Kleinman, head of portfolio services and marketing at Obvious, says that they don't like to use the term 'impact investing', as that can be associated with charity or doing good as opposed to superior investment returns. Instead, he says, 'We are investing in companies that are reimagining trillion-dollar sectors in the economy and we believe they will outperform their peers.' He says that in 2014, when Obvious was founded, it was unusual for a venture capitalist to stress that it was trying to do good as well as make money. 'This wasn't common even six years ago where, if a venture capitalist walked into the room and led with purpose, they would have been walked out. It was a contrarian philosophy,' he says.

The role of the battery

One key issue is the cost of the battery used in an electric car. Both the production of the battery itself and the raw materials used to manufacture it currently make electric vehicles more expensive. But battery prices have been falling rapidly. A 2019 report from Bloomberg New Energy Finance – which also predicted that electric vehicles would cost the same on average as standard ones by 2025 – noted that a lithium-ion battery's average price fell 18 per cent from 2017 to 2018. Since 2010, the price had fallen 85 per cent, and the report predicted that by 2030, the batteries will cost a third of what they did in 2018.

Yet lithium-ion batteries are not without their complications. The raw materials used in them are not always extracted ethically. A DNV GL report warned that production of lithium-ion batteries was straining the world's supply of cobalt: with over 55 per cent of global reserves in the Democratic Republic of Congo, there were supply concerns as well as environmental and sustainability issues associated with the mining process.

A *Global EV Outlook* report in 2019 suggested that

governments should allocate funds to accelerate research and innovation in advanced lithium-ion and solid-state battery technologies – the latter being smaller, cheaper and longer-lived than standard lithium-ion batteries. Toyota had planned to use the 2020 Olympics in Japan to debut an electric vehicle using a solid-state battery before the event was cancelled due to the coronavirus. Car companies as well as venture capitalists have been investing in battery start-ups. These include Sila Nanotechnologies, backed by BMW, Daimler and the Canada Pension Plan Investment Board, and QuantumScape, whose investors include Volkswagen and Bill Gates's Breakthrough Energy Ventures fund. Breakthrough has also backed Lilac, a mining technology company that is looking to improve lithium extraction processes.

Then there is the question of the source of the electricity used to power electric vehicles. Ideally this would be green as well. Michael Bruun, the Goldman Sachs partner who took a stake in Orsted, also took a stake in Swedish company Northvolt, which produces batteries that are 100 per cent hydropowered. 'With Dong we said we were backing the world's leading offshore wind energy company. I think that was thought-provoking at the time because nobody knew about it. Similarly with Northvolt we said we're backing the world's first green energy battery company,' he explains. BMW and Volkswagen also invested in Northvolt, which said at the time of its 2019 fund-raising that it would use the money to build Europe's largest lithium-ion battery plant, to begin production in 2021.

Some people are investing in green hydrogen batteries. Green hydrogen is made by converting wind or solar electricity into hydrogen through electrolysis, while blue hydrogen is produced from fossil fuels. In 2019, Trafigura, one of the world's top commodity trading houses, took a stake in German start-up Hy2gen AG, which builds green hydrogen production facilities. Yet other investors warn that hydrogen fuel cell technology is an area where there is a lot of 'hype'. Christian Roessing, manager of the Pictet Clean Energy fund, says that the interest in certain smaller companies in this field reminds him of the solar boom in the noughties that ended in tears for so many companies and investors. The Motley Fool, an investment website, argued in March 2020 that Ballard Power, for example, a hydrogen fuel cell company that had seen huge swings in its share price, was a stock 'investors should probably steer clear of unless they have a tremendous appetite for risk and a firm belief that fuel cells will catch on sooner rather than later'. There were also signs that such companies might struggle in the low oil price environment triggered by the coronavirus market crash in 2020, with hydrogen fuel cells looking like a cost-effective alternative when the price of oil is high, but not so much when it's cheap.

Helping electric vehicles to get around

Infrastructure is another key challenge when it comes to electric transportation. The UK government promised that every driver would live within 30 miles of a charging point come 2035 – meaning that a huge number of electric points need to be installed. In Germany, car companies have been putting pressure on the government to accelerate the installation of charging points and increase financial incentives for emission-free cars to boost demand. The Bloomberg New Energy Finance report notes that a patchwork of solutions is emerging to address the charging issue: including ultra-fast chargers, wireless charging and the sort of battery swapping used by Gogoro. Yet although many drivers will have access to charging stations at home or at work, the challenge will be how to service those who have neither. 'If, through technology innovation and government policy, EV charging barriers are significantly lowered, adoption could be faster in the 2030s,' the report states.

A 2018 report by Wood Mackenzie predicted that 12 million residential charging points and 1.2 million public points would be established in the US by 2030; worldwide, it predicted that nearly 40 million would be installed over that period. That sort of growth, it said, would require utility companies as well as oil and gas companies and other specialists to test new business models and engage with people to find solutions.

Private equity funds are among the backers of start-up companies in EV infrastructure. One of these, London-based Zouk Capital, is a lead investor in EO and InstaVolt, two electric vehicle charging point companies. As with many of the companies discussed in this book, investors in start-up EV infrastructure companies can hope to see them bought by bigger companies, yielding healthy profits for the early-stage investors. Oil and gas companies, for example, are getting in on the action as part of their plans to embrace the energy transition. Chargemaster, a supplier of infrastructure for electric vehicle charging, was snapped up by BP in 2018 and installs charging points for local authorities across the UK. It also has contracts with leading car companies, including BMW and Toyota, to install chargers in people's homes. Draper Esprit, one of Europe's largest tech-focused venture capital firms, sold its stake in Pod Point in February 2020, saying it had more than doubled its money in three years. EDF Energy, the French-owned utility company, was the buyer. US-based Chargepoint, which claims to have the largest network of charging points in the world, raised money from investors including the Canada Pension Plan Investment Board, Texan-based private equity firm Quantum Energy Partners, and Chevron Technology Ventures, the corporate venture capital arm of Chevron.

Biofuels and aviation

Biofuels were initially thought to be a game changer when they arrived on the scene in the mid 1980s. But it's now clear that they pose problems as a renewable energy source: they can cause forests or wetlands to be converted to agricultural land, increasing emissions and offsetting any benefits that they bring as an alternative fuel. As a result, the EU has now restricted the use of biofuel in transport that can be counted as renewable energy to just 7 per cent.

But biofuels are proving attractive in the aviation industry. Flights make up more than 2 per cent of global greenhouse gas emissions – or at least they did before the 2020 pandemic grounded airlines. This means that if global aviation were a country, it would rank in the top 10 emitters. It remains to be seen how long it will take for aviation to match its pre-pandemic emissions, with many airlines warning that they will not see a recovery to 2019 levels of activity for years to come. An EU report from 2019 notes that, while sustainable aviation fuels such as electrofuels (which, if produced from renewable electricity, are potentially zero emission) have the potential to significantly reduce emissions, their use is minimal and likely to remain limited in the short term. Part of the problem is that few demonstrator projects have been undertaken, as production costs are high.

Biofuels are already well established: planes have been mixing them with more conventional fuels since 2008, when Virgin Atlantic first flew a jet from London to Amsterdam to prove the technology worked. Once made from unsustainable sources like palm oil, biofuels are now looking at more sustainable sources like waste oils from biological origin or agricultural residues and even household waste. Most planes can currently take blends of up to 50 per cent biofuels but Rolls-Royce is working on newer engines that can take up to 100 per cent sustainable fuel.

Biofuels are still significantly more expensive than conventional fuels. The cost needs to come down to make them viable, and this is where innovation comes in. Companies including US-based World Energy and Finland's Neste are producing low-carbon aviation fuels on a commercial scale, with others in the pipeline. World Energy is a good example of a new-technology company that has attracted attention from a family office: in 2018 it received a $345m investment from Canadian family office CFFI, headed by billionaire John Risley, whose wealth came from founding Clearwater Fine Foods, one of the largest seafood businesses in the world.

British Airways is working with the start-up Velocys to build a UK plant to convert waste into sustainable aviation fuel, having invested in the company in 2019 along with Shell. Velocys is listed on London's alternative investment market; one of its major investors is Russian oil billionaire and Chelsea football club owner Roman Abramovich, through his investment company Ervington Investments.

Others are looking at hydrogen solutions for aviation. Jeremy Oppenheim's Systemiq, which acts as both a consultant and an investor in early-stage ventures in the climate space, is helping US company ZeroAvia to expand in Europe with the help of a UK government grant. Its hydrogen fuel cell aims to deliver the same performance as a conventional aircraft engine, but with zero carbon emissions and half the operating costs.

Another alternative gas under consideration is green ammonia, which could be used more frequently in ships. Shipping too is a big beast in transport emissions, accounting for 2.5 per cent of global carbon dioxide emissions and up to 3 per cent of greenhouse gases, according to the International Council on Clean Transportation (ICCT). The International Maritime Organization has set a goal of halving the industry's 2008 level of greenhouse gas emissions by 2050. Samsung Heavy Industries and MAN Energy Solutions, among others, are backing a project to produce an ammonia-fuelled tanker by 2024. Toyota and Hyundai have also been looking into manufacturing ammonia–hydrogen-fuelled cars as an alternative to conventional electric vehicles.

What can you do?

- Low-risk investors: look at transport funds or energy or climate change funds that have interesting holdings in transport. The Pictet Clean Energy fund is investing in NXP Semiconductors, while the Schroders Climate Change fund is investing in BMW, for example. These funds have the advantage of doing the legwork for you, but they may also invest in other things besides transport. Always check the top 10 holdings of a fund to make sure you're happy with the fund manager's selection.
- Medium-risk investors: those who wish to move beyond mutual funds could build a select

portfolio of single blue-chip companies: mainstream transport companies with good dividends and strong earnings that are investing in electric vehicles, such as BMW, identified by the Schroders Climate Change fund as a leader in the field. Bear in mind that while such an approach avoids fund management costs and can give you a more targeted portfolio, picking your own stocks concentrates your risk.

- High-risk investors: cleantech is where it's at again in transport. Hydrogen fuel cell start-ups are attracting venture capital, for example, and buying shares in a venture capital or private equity fund with holdings in electric vehicles is a way for higher-risk investors to gain access with the promise of higher returns.

7

Farms of the Future:
Investing in Agriculture

Josh Tetrick was studying sociology at Cornell
University when he was faced with the question, as he
puts it, of 'What the hell am I going to do with my
life?' Half of his friends really cared about society and
were headed for a career with NGOs. The other half
wanted to work in finance, with an eventual goal of
giving some money away. Neither option felt quite
right to Tetrick. 'There was something about the
whole non-profit world that never entirely appealed to
me: it always felt slow, overly bureaucratic. It didn't
feel like it was on the bleeding edge of getting stuff
done. It also didn't appeal to me to spend my life
doing something I didn't feel was meaningful.' He
ended up working in sub-Saharan Africa, where he
witnessed extreme poverty first hand for the first time.
He also read a book called *Fortune is at the Bottom of the
Pyramid*, which argued that the biggest opportunities
for multinational companies in emerging markets were

in raising people out of poverty, and he started thinking that if you wanted to change things for the better, the most effective way to do it was through business.

Tetrick liked the idea of focusing on food as a way of solving society's problems, as it had what he called multiplier effects: it could deal with obesity, help with malnutrition, create jobs and help mitigate climate change. As it happened, his best friend, Josh Balk, had long been interested in animal welfare and was a director for food policy at the US Humane Society, which lobbies for battery hens to be made cage-free. The two decided to team up, and in 2011 they founded Hampton Creek, a food technology company that would focus on vegan egg substitutes. Disruptive companies are those that invent something new that will eventually replace established products in their field. At the time, the idea of a disruptive food company was something new for many investors. According to Balk: 'Hampton Creek was one of the first companies in the space so what it did was break through the investment world for these large firms to start looking at food. Before, they were looking at cleantech companies. Facebook is disruptive: how can a food company be disruptive? What Hampton Creek did was break the mould and say: hey, we had an idea.'

As of June 2020, the company, like so many other private start-ups, was not yet profitable. But by 2016, it was valued at over $1bn, giving it the coveted unicorn status.

Yet while Hampton Creek – since rebranded as Just – has a good story behind it, it also serves as a cautionary tale of how even the best ideas for companies with the best intentions may not translate into success. Tetrick has been the subject of various investigation-style pieces in the media. The *Atlantic* wrote in 2017 that Hampton Creek had been 'besieged by federal investigations, product withdrawals, and an exodus of top leadership'. A *Bloomberg Businessweek* article in 2016, entitled 'How Hampton Creek sold Silicon Valley on a fake-mayo miracle', quoted former employees claiming that they had been asked to buy the alternative mayo products themselves to inflate sales.

Without (presumably) referring to his own company, Tetrick says: 'Companies that are attempting to solve problems are just like companies that are not solving problems in that some can be extraordinary and some can suck.' If companies are trying to achieve socially responsible outcomes but in a wrong-headed way, he says, 'you'd be better off donating to a non-profit than investing in that company'. But he also admits that Just, in particular, made mistakes along the way. 'We've had to learn how to be a more mature company, how to focus more, how to do fewer things, how to execute the boring things around sourcing and the tactical work of building a brand and intelligent R&D. That's not about ESG or impact metrics or the personal satisfaction of doing an enormous amount of good, it's about the real hard unsexy grind of building a company no matter what the industry it's in.'

Investors have still been happy to buy into Just. Tetrick says that shareholders include the Heineken family, Japanese conglomerate Mitsui, sovereign wealth funds including Singapore's Temasek, and early-stage venture capital funds including veteran investor Peter Thiel's Founders Fund. Some of them want a stable source of wealth over the very long term (in the case of Temasek for the citizens of Singapore); others are keen to invest in companies that are attempting to solve environmental problems (in the case of various family offices whose younger members want to change the world); while some simply want to have their finger on the pulse of emerging technologies (in the case of various high-net-worth individuals; the minimum investment in Just, as for many private early-stage companies, is about $1m).

All these investors are hoping to have picked the next big thing in alternative food. And that is because food is another area that is undergoing huge innovation and development in response to climate change. Agriculture makes up 11 per cent of global greenhouse gas emissions. The sector is not an offender on the same level as energy and transport, but it is significant nonetheless. And it has associated effects – land-use change and forestry account for a further 6 per cent of emissions, with clearing forests to use for agricultural purposes a big factor in that category.

In fact, taking into account other associated activities like storage, transport, packaging, retail, consumption and food waste, the food system accounts for 21–37 per cent of total greenhouse gas emissions, according to the Intergovernmental Panel on Climate Change (IPCC), which says that, as a result, agriculture and the food system 'are key to global climate change responses'. It recommends that more efficient production, transport and processing on the supply side should be combined with modification of food choices and reducing food waste on the demand side.

As we shall see, various new technologies and practices are emerging to help solve some of these issues, and investors are getting involved.

The rise of the vegan

The most high-profile areas in which changes in food production are taking place because of climate change are alternative meat and veganism. That is something that Just and many other food companies are seeking to tap into. The IPCC report doesn't call for everyone in the world to become a vegan, but it notes that balanced diets featuring plant-based foods and sustainable low-carbon-producing animal-sourced food present 'major opportunities' for adapting to and mitigating climate change.

A letter published in science magazine *BioScience* and signed by 11,000 scientists warning of the effects of climate change said that eating mostly plant-based foods and fewer animal products could significantly lower greenhouse gas emissions as well as improve human health. It could also free up croplands for growing human plant food instead of livestock feed, while making grazing land available to plant more trees.

Sales of plant-based products in the US (plant-based is sometimes used as a synonym for vegan) were up more than 11 per cent in 2019, compared to just 2.2 per cent growth in the overall US retail food market. Plant-based milk was one of the most popular categories, making up 14 per cent of the entire US milk category, with sales up 5 per cent in 2019 while cow's milk sales were nearly flat.

Of course, it is not necessary to be a vegan or vegetarian to eat plant-based food, and despite the hype, the proportion of people identifying as vegan in the UK, for example, was still only 1 per cent at the start of 2020. The biggest shift has been the rise in flexitarianism, whereby meat-eaters simply try to eat less meat to help reduce their carbon footprint. While the founder of Impossible Foods has said his goal is to replace animal foods altogether by 2035, Beyond Meat has said it is targeting mainstream consumers who simply want to eat less meat.

The number of Britons trying out meat-free foods rose from 50 per cent in 2017 to 65 per cent in 2019, according to market intelligence agency Mintel. Sales of meat-free food grew 40 per cent over the five years to 2020, and Mintel expects UK sales to rise by another

34 per cent at least by 2024. The proportion of meat-eaters who reduced or limited the amount of meat they consumed rose from 28 per cent in 2017 to 39 per cent in 2019.

There were also signs that the coronavirus pandemic would prove a boon for plant-based alternatives. With meatpacking factories shut down across the US and labour shortages affecting production, plant-based factories, where production is more automated, saw less disruption in their supply chains. US sales of plant-based meat substitutes jumped by 265 per cent over an eight-week period, according to consumer data group Nielsen, compared with rises of just 39 per cent for fresh meat.

This change in consumer behaviour means that plant-based foods represent an opportunity, and mainstream food companies have been getting in on the act. In 2017, McDonald's introduced a McVegan burger in Sweden and then Finland, and has faced calls from celebrities and pressure groups to do the same in other countries.

Yet just as fossil fuel companies trying to brandish their renewables credentials led to some awkward advertising campaigns, some food companies trying to ride the vegan wave have also run into difficulties. In April 2020, a campaign by Burger King was banned by the UK advertising watchdog for implying that its Rebel Whopper, described in the ad as the chain's first plant-based burger, was suitable for vegans and vegetarians, when it was not. The company was already facing a lawsuit from a vegan man in the US who argued that it had mis-marketed its Impossible Whopper burgers as suitable for vegans even though they were cooked on the same grill as meat products.

Yet the small but growing trend towards plant-based foods in the West is competing with a rise in meat consumption in emerging markets as people get richer and can afford it. That is leading to an overall increase in meat consumption on a global scale, with an average rise of 1.9 per cent a year in the decade to 2017, according to the UN Food and Agriculture Organization.

Eating less meat is one way that consumers have been addressing this issue. But there is also money to be made by investing in companies that are trying to become the next big thing in alternative meat. Perhaps the biggest success story in the plant-based food trend so far is that of Beyond Meat, which makes plant-based burgers from pea proteins. The company listed on the stock market in 2019 in what was one of the most wildly successful initial public offerings of the year. An article in the *Financial Times* said that many early investors in Beyond Meat were 'sitting on eye-watering gains' after the company was valued at $1.3bn privately but rose to a market capitalisation of $12bn. Those early investors included venture capital firms such as Kleiner Perkins and Obvious Ventures, as well as Morgan Creek Capital Management and Union Grove Venture Partners.

Investment in innovative food start-ups doubled in 2019 to hit more than $1bn, according to venture capital firm AgFunder's 2019 agri-food tech investment report. That was helped by a $300m fund-raising by Impossible Foods, a rival to Beyond Meat, which attracted investment from a range of venture capitalists as well as celebrities, including Jay-Z, Katy Perry and Serena Williams.

Just like energy and transport start-ups, innovative food start-ups are not only aiming to list on the stock exchange. Some are being snapped up by bigger, more established companies in their sector that are looking to diversify and position themselves to profit from new technologies in a climate change era. While Burger King partnered with Impossible Foods to make its meat-free burger in the US, it chose to partner with Unilever when it launched the Rebel Whopper in Europe. That was because Unilever had in 2018 bought Dutch company The Vegetarian Butcher, which was founded in 2007 by Jaap Korteweg, a ninth-generation meat farmer who became a vegetarian and wanted to create food, as Unilever put it, that could satisfy his need for quality 'meat'. Purchases like that helped Unilever to top the rankings in a 2019 report by the CDP of consumer companies that were best prepared for climate change and a low-carbon economy.

Agribusiness Cargill, one of the world's largest privately held companies, has also muscled in on the action, launching plant-based hamburgers and 'fake meat' products in April, while Tyson, one of the biggest meat producers, made a surprise entry into the market in 2019 as it announced a new plant-based brand, Raised and Rooted.

Josh Balk notes how disruptive the plant-based industry is proving to be for traditional food companies.

'The meat industry certainly knows plant based has arrived. [If you had told me that] the largest advertiser of plant-based meat is Burger King . . . a year ago I'd have said you were crazy. When you see meat companies, fast food companies, family dining chains [offering plant-based food], you know the time has come that this is mainstream.'

Just as some oil and gas companies are pivoting to renewable energy, like Denmark's Orsted, some meat companies are turning to plant-based food. In 2017, Maple Leaf, a major packaged meat producer in Canada, bought two plant-based companies, Lightlife and Field Roast, and in 2020 it unveiled plans to build the biggest plant-based factory in the US. Now the company says it wants to become the most sustainable protein company on earth, through a combination of fewer artificial ingredients, better care for animals, and reducing its carbon footprint.

But with hype can come overvaluation. Just as some investors fear that hydrogen fuel cell companies are too expensive, some watched the rise of Beyond Meat's share price with caution. After peaking at $230 a share in July 2019, for example, the stock subsequently fell to below $100 by October that year, meaning that anyone who had bought in at the top of the market, when enthusiasm was at its highest, would have lost more than half their money in just three months. Short sellers – investors betting that shares will fall in value rather than rise – began to target Beyond Meat as a result. And analysts warned that alternative meat was a market where there were low barriers to entry, meaning that rivals to Beyond Meat, particularly bigger, more established food groups like Nestlé or Kellogg with more money to spend on research and development, could reduce its potential to dominate the market.

THE CELL-BASED START-UP

In a small room at a law firm in the City of London around 40 well-heeled people, mostly women, sit around at the end of a weekday. At the front stands Benjamina Bollag, the co-founder of Higher Steaks, a cell-based meat company. Her job is to convince the angel investors in the room – part of Angel Academe, a female-driven network that aims to fund companies started by women in recognition of the fact that men are more likely to secure early-stage funding – to invest. She explains how the company is experimenting with a technique where cells are taken from a living pig without harming the animal then grown in a lab. Unlike plant-based alternatives to meat, this is the real thing – sort of.

Higher Steaks is one of a growing number of start-ups that are trying to make lab-grown foods as a way of addressing climate change, food shortages and animal welfare all in one go. While there were just two such companies as recently as 2016, by 2020 there were more than 60 start-ups, though none of their products had yet to hit the supermarket shelves. Bollag's company focuses on pork. She has been looking for a £2.7m investment, but explains during the presentation that a US-based family office with a particular interest in alternative food has agreed to chip in more than £2m. There are questions from the floor. One woman asks about the 'gross-out factor': will consumers, wary of genetically modified crops, really accept lab-grown meat? It's a fair point: a 2019 survey by US marketing firm Charleston Orwig on 'synthetic' or 'lab-grown' foods such as cell-based meat found that 40 per cent of respondents said the products were 'scary'. Younger consumers, though, aged between 18 and 24, were significantly more interested in trying the foods compared to those aged 65 and older. But overall the mood in the room is positive, and many of the angel investors sign up afterwards to find out more.

Farming

Producing different types of food that are less carbon intensive is one approach to reducing emissions produced in agriculture. Another is to focus on farming itself: how existing food is produced and whether this process can be made more efficient and less carbon intensive. Companies that are trying to solve this issue tend to be referred to as agtech or agritech companies. Just as the use of technology to create plant-based food or meat alternatives was behind the wider curve, with clean energy tech much more established, agritech is also seen as a latecomer to the field of climate change technology. David Perry, head of agricultural microbes start-up Indigo, told the *Financial Times* in 2018 that while Amazon had disrupted retail, Tesla had disrupted transport and Netflix had disrupted media, agriculture was 'the last of the large industries to really adopt new technologies and business models'.

Enter precision agriculture, or precision farming methods. These use technology including drones, satellites, robots and mass-scale data collection to help farmers make sure that each plant gets the right amount of water and fertiliser, increasing productivity and reducing the environmental impacts of farming. One example is Farmobile, a data technology company that helps farmers to improve efficiency and profitability. One of its investors is Anterra Capital, an Amsterdam- and Boston-based venture capital firm focused on food and agriculture. Or there is Trimble Navigation – one of whose shareholders is UK environmental investment specialist Impax Asset Management – which produces software to make agriculture more efficient, and has also started applying its software to other sectors, such as construction.

Other agtech companies are trying to reduce the use of pesticides, which contribute to greenhouse gas emissions, but in a way that allows farms to use technology to improve their crop yields. Organic farming, which also eschews chemical pesticides, is well established, but farms that practise it tend to be less productive on average, with a lower yield that makes the produce more expensive to consumers. In addition to being less efficient in terms of feeding a growing population around the world, that means organic farming could also require more land, which would have the knock-on negative effect of needing more forests to be cleared. This is where agtech companies can step in. Canadian agtech start-up Terramera uses technology to make natural pesticides more effective than their synthetic counterparts. It aims to reduce chemical use by 80 per cent and increase yields by 20 per cent in the next decade.

And just as some meat is being grown in labs, some farming is going inside too. This is a trend known as vertical farming, in which crops are grown not in a flat field or greenhouse but on shelves one above the other in converted warehouses or shipping containers. It yields more crops per square metre than traditional farming, uses less water and isn't subject to seasonal weather variations so can keep going all year round. Vertical farming also has the advantage of reducing food miles and the need to import crops, something that could become more valuable in the post-coronavirus era.

Crop One Holdings, which in 2018 announced plans to build the largest vertical farm in the world in a joint venture with Emirates Flight Catering in Dubai, says that it uses 95–99 per cent less water than conventional farming. Growing Underground grows greens in London's abandoned Tube train tunnels, using a hydroponic system that needs 70 per cent less water than traditional farming. One of its investors is Unreasonable Group, which is an unusual organisation in that it both invests and acts as an adviser to entrepreneurs as well as connecting them with other investors through its network. Another company that Unreasonable supports is Kiverdi, which uses technology to convert carbon dioxide into food, building on technology used to create food in space for NASA astronauts.

Currently, however, vertical farming uses up considerably more energy in the form of electricity than other types of farming due to the need for artificial lighting and climate-control systems, meaning that this is still a barrier to many companies achieving profitability.

Food waste

Changing consumer behaviour in terms of what we eat is one approach to food and climate change. Changing behaviour in terms of *how* we eat is another. Food waste is a big issue when it comes to overall global emissions. It's not only the waste of resources: the crops grown that weren't eaten, the cows killed without even being consumed. It's also the methane that the food waste releases back into the atmosphere, particularly when it's thrown into landfill rather than recycled. Right now, the world wastes between 25 and 30 per cent of the food it produces. That waste accounted for 8–10 per cent of total greenhouse gas emissions between 2010 and 2016, according to the IPCC. This could be remedied not just by consumer awareness and behaviour, but also by processes: improved harvesting techniques, on-farm storage, infrastructure, transport and packaging.

Winnow, a UK start-up, uses technology to help restaurant kitchens minimise their food waste. The company estimates that some commercial kitchens waste up to 20 per cent of the food they buy. It uses artificial intelligence to take photos of food that is thrown away and identify which dishes it comes from – which food consumers aren't eating as much of – to help the chefs make better choices about what to serve. Kitchens using Winnow tend to see a 40–70 per cent reduction in food waste within 6–12 months, the company says. In 2019 it raised $12m from a pool of investors that included the Ingka Group, IKEA's parent company.

There are also apps for food waste that are attracting interest from investors. Too Good to Go is a Copenhagen-based app which connects people with food that shops and restaurants would otherwise have thrown away. It was founded in 2015 and largely backed by angel investors.

Other companies are focusing on changing how food is packaged. Food Freshness Technology aims to extend the shelf life of fruit and vegetables both in supermarkets and at home by providing packaging that ensures freshness for longer and is also itself sustainably made. Its investors include Anterra Capital.

Food waste is a good transition into the final thematic

chapter in this book, on energy efficiency. For any business, being more efficient is a way of saving energy and money and improving profits. So it's an area where climate change goals and natural business development can be nicely aligned. As we'll see, investing in technology to make companies more energy efficient is hugely important when it comes to reshaping the economy for the future.

What can you do?

- Low-risk investors: there are a few funds focused on sustainable food and nutrition that will invest mainly in listed companies. These include the Smart Food fund from BNP Paribas, the Nutrition fund from Pictet, the Food and Agricultural Opportunities fund from Sarasin, and the RobecoSAM Sustainable Food Equities fund. As always, check what the top holdings of any mutual fund are before deciding you're happy with it.
- Medium-risk investors: a 'best in class' approach could be taken here by looking for large, listed consumer or food companies that are investing in alternative foods and trying to pivot their businesses to take advantage of this growing market. Think Unilever or Kellogg: strong companies that tend to weather recessions better than other types of company but

that are helping the alternative food market to grow.

- High-risk investors: food technology or agritech start-ups are where it's at when it comes to investing in food to solve climate change. Beyond Meat was the first major alternative food producer to list on the stock market, in 2019, and many more are expected to follow. Start-ups looking to produce meat substitutes abound, and not all will be winners. But many need capital from venture capitalists or angel investors.

8

The Circular Economy:
Investing in Energy Efficiency

James Purcell was the head of sustainable and impact investing at the wealth management division of UBS, a Swiss bank boasting some of the world's richest people as clients, when he started to notice some trends emerging among the wealthy clients he was advising. They all wanted to invest their money in a positive way, but the sorts of things they wanted to invest in often related back to their personal consumer habits. Like a lot of environmentally minded rich people, they drove Teslas, so they wanted to know about investing in electric vehicles. They were also trying to eat less meat, or even turning vegan, so they wanted to know about investing in plant-based food companies.

We've looked at the trend among the wealthy to invest in environmental solutions. But what Purcell noticed was that they were too often skewing their investment ideas to their personal experience. 'People gravitate to things they're familiar with so they're more likely to end up with investments in consumer goods than industrial applications,' he notes. This is understandable. Investing in electric cars or alternative meat, to put it bluntly, sounds more exciting than, say, investing in a semiconductor equipment manufacturer. Consumers are familiar with the notion of trying to save energy at home. Turning off lights when not in use or using the energy-saving cycle on the washing machine are fairly ingrained practices among the standard environmentally aware citizen. Yet we don't often give much thought to the technical side of how saving energy comes about. In fact, energy efficiency in industrial processes, in buildings and across companies in general, is another crucial way of reducing emissions across the economy.

Energy efficiency

In 2018, improvements in energy efficiency saw what the International Energy Agency called a 'historic slow-down' and the lowest rate of improvement since the start of the decade. It was driven, it said, in part by a rise in industrial production in the US and China, but also by hot weather in the US that saw a rise in energy use from air conditioners. As cars themselves became more effi-cient, consumers preferred larger models, while ve-hicle occupancy rates fell. Residential buildings were built to better standards but residents themselves were using more devices and living in bigger homes. Yet the International Energy Agency says that a sharp pickup in energy-efficiency improvements is key to keeping emissions rising less than 2 per cent above pre-industrial levels by 2050, as discussed in the Paris Agreement, with savings in industry, transport and buildings the main sectors to work on.

Governments have a larger role to play here than perhaps in any other sector discussed in this book, as regulations are vital in setting standards for emissions of products or activities. The non-profit American Council for an Energy-Efficient Economy has ranked countries according to how energy efficient they are and found various differences: as of its most recent report, in 2018, Germany ranks the highest for national efforts, as well as ranking joint highest overall with Italy, while France led on transportation, Spain on buildings-related efforts and Japan on industry. The UK ranked fourth overall, while the US had slipped since 2016 from eighth to tenth place. As more regulations are introduced, companies will of course look for the products that can help them achieve more efficiency – and this is where investors come in.

Investing in energy-efficient technology might be hard for the average investor to get excited about unless, perhaps, they have an engineering degree. The companies' own descriptions of themselves are often eye-wateringly technical. Tomra Systems, a Norwegian company in the top 10 holdings of the Candriam SRI Equity Climate

Action fund, for example, says that it 'creates sensor-based solutions for optimal resource productivity'. In plainer terms, the company uses technology to collect, sort and minimise waste in the food, recycling and mining industries.

Yet the good news is that often energy-efficient companies are easier to access for investors. Many, like Tomra, are already large listed firms as opposed to start-ups using new technology, as is often the case with alternative meat or hydrogen fuel cell companies. And investing in energy efficiency doesn't have to involve new technology; it can include bog-standard stuff like waste management and recycling. Jon Forster, a fund manager at Impax Asset Management, argues that these are also 'pretty powerful themes' that will give investors good diversification in their portfolios. His Impax Environmental Markets fund has about a third of its holdings in energy efficiency, for example. 'We've always said a much more compelling way of dealing with climate change is energy efficiency – it's not generating cleaner power; it's using less of it,' he says.

There are various quite specific areas that climate change funds focusing on energy efficiency are attracted to. One is semiconductor companies. 'The best weapon we have to reduce power consumption is power semiconductors,' argues Christian Roessing, manager of the Pictet Clean Energy fund. His fund holds Chinese-listed NXP Semiconductors and ON Semiconductor, a US-listed Fortune 500 company that uses semiconductor technology to make various processes across industry and transport more efficient. Another of the fund's biggest holdings is Applied Materials, a US-listed company that is the largest supplier of materials to the semiconductor industry, as well as the solar photovoltaic (PV) industry. The Candriam fund also lists ON Semiconductor as one of its top 10 holdings.

As more and more people use the Internet, power-guzzling data centres that support computing and cloud technology are also coming under scrutiny. The Pictet fund invests in Equinix, a data centre that aims to power itself exclusively through renewable energy and has high energy-efficiency standards.

Some fund managers are investing in weight reduction across various industries: a key way to reduce energy usage. If cars or aeroplanes, for example, are made of lighter materials, it will require less energy to move them about. Often, software companies are helping industrial companies to do this. 'We've seen a shift within industrials from hardware to software that is making those industries more energy-efficient,' notes Roessing. Software from Ansys, for example, can be used to simulate models to help people design things more efficiently without having to create physical prototypes. That can mean, for example, that they are able to work out which parts of a plane need to be crafted out of stronger, heavier materials like steel, and which parts can just be plastic, which is lighter, thus hugely improving the energy efficiency of the vehicle. Investing in companies like this, says Roessing, broadens the definition of what a clean energy fund would have been 10 years ago. There are start-up options in lightweight materials as well. Prime Coalition has backed Mallinda, a Colorado-based start-up that makes recyclable, remouldable plastics that can be used, for example, in car parts, making the weight of the car less and hence reducing the amount of energy required to power it.

Building energy efficiency

An additional bonus for energy-efficiency solutions is that they save companies money. In a post-coronavirus world where the economy is struggling, fund managers are betting that energy efficiency will be more rather than less valued. The first half of 2020 saw institutional investors urging governments around the world to prioritise sustainability in their economic recovery plans. German asset manager DWS, for example, specifically recommended that governments focus on investments into energy efficiency in buildings. Developing climate and energy standards for existing buildings and aligning incentives between building owners and tenants was key, according to Roelfien Kuijpers, head of responsible investments at DWS, in a statement put out by the Institutional Investors Group on Climate Change.

The buildings and construction sectors combined are responsible for over one third of global final energy consumption and nearly 40 per cent of total direct and indirect CO_2 emissions, according to the IEA. Two thirds of countries lacked mandatory building energy codes in 2018, meaning that more than three billion square metres were built without mandatory performance requirements that year. Governments are taking steps in this regard: eight European cities, including Dublin, Leeds and Warsaw, have set a zero emissions target for their existing buildings stock by 2050, as part of an EU-funded scheme aimed at showing that net zero is possible for buildings in urban environments. The IEA says that enormous potential to cut emissions remains untapped due to the widespread use of less efficient technologies, a lack of effective policies and insufficient investment in sustainable buildings. The agency has called for all countries to introduce mandatory building energy codes; but of course investors can get involved too.

There are all sorts of subsectors of building and construction where technology can help to improve energy efficiency. One of the biggest is air conditioners. Using air conditioners and electric fans to stay cool accounts for nearly 20 per cent of the total electricity used in buildings around the world, yet for cost reasons most people purchase new air conditioners that are two to three times less efficient than the best available model. The IEA's chief executive has called the growing demand for air conditioners – the use of which is expected to soar over the next three decades to become one of the top drivers of global electricity demand – 'one of the most critical blind spots' in the energy debate. Most homes in hot countries have not yet purchased their first AC unit, but sales are rising rapidly in emerging economies. To put that in context, the IEA says that without action to address energy efficiency, energy demand for space cooling will more than triple by 2050 – consuming as much electricity as all of China and India today.

The IEA has called on governments to set higher standards for energy efficiency, but innovation in the private sector is already taking place, and investors are getting involved. One California-based start-up, Treau, is developing energy-efficient, environmentally friendly air-conditioning units for use in the home, and is backed by Prime Coalition. More broadly under the building category, Kingspan, an Irish company that specialises in energy-efficient insulation, has also been a favourite of environmentally minded funds.

THE NEXT-GEN INVESTOR

Liesel Pritzker Simmons inherited her fortune as a member of America's Pritzker family, and is one of a number of prominent so-called 'next-gen' investors interested in making an impact with her wealth. While she and her friends in the impact space have been investing in climate change solutions for some time, she thinks the wider investment community is at a tipping point. 'It's not an ideological choice any more, which business has been slow at realising. It's a financial choice,' she says. She believes that a lot of investors are afraid to back new technologies, remembering the cleantech crash of 2007–8 in which so many venture capitalists lost money. 'They're not actually talking about disrupting the air conditioner, which is actually what we need to do. We've been stifled and are not thinking big enough in terms of what is investable,' she says. 'If you make air conditioners and are able to make the cheapest and most energy-efficient air conditioner the world has ever seen you're going to win: regulation will move in that direction and demand for air con will go up.'

In 2020, Pritzker Simmons was planning to reorient her whole portfolio 'with a climate lens'. That didn't necessarily mean adding risk, or investing in earlier-stage companies with unproven technologies, though she does wish investors and big companies would do more to support research and development. She believes that mitigation – stopping climate change from getting worse – and adaptation – looking at how we will adapt to climate change – are important themes as well as the innovation and bold bets needed from investors.

The circular economy

The 'circular economy' describes waste that is reused, recycled or repurposed further down the line. Shoe manufacturer Timberland, for example, has partnered with a tyre company to produce shoes from old tyres. The failure to repurpose single-use plastics is widely recognised as a problem by any environmentally minded consumer. But investors are now starting to scrutinise other areas of the economy too. A 2019 paper from the European Commission identifies eight priority areas for a circular economy: in addition to textiles, it lists packaging, food, furniture, electrical and electronic equipment and batteries, transport, building and construction, and chemicals. And the world is not getting any more circular. According to the Circularity Gap report published in Davos in 2020, it is only 8.6 per cent circular, down from 9.1 per cent two years previously.

The Ellen MacArthur Foundation – set up by the eponymous UK sailor specifically to promote the idea of the circular economy – calculates that renewable energy and energy efficiency only account for 55 per cent of global emissions. The remaining 45 per cent of emissions are associated with making products, and circular-economy strategies applied to the four key industrial materials of cement, steel, plastic and aluminium could help reduce emissions by 40 per cent by 2050.

Fund managers at the Impax Environmental Markets fund argue that a 'new front' is opening in the campaign to create a circular economy, in the form of textiles. Creating fabric uses a huge amount of water and land and can lead to considerable pollution. The European Environment Agency says that textiles is the fourth highest category, after food, housing and transport, for use of primary raw materials and water, and the fifth highest for greenhouse gas emissions. It argues that reducing the environmental footprint of textiles will require 'a systemic change towards circularity' and wide-scale implementation of circular business models. As a result, the Impax Environmental Markets fund has bought a stake in Austrian company Lenzing, which produces man-made fibres that are less resource-intensive.

Other companies are homing in on less obvious areas in need of a little circularity. Royal DSM, the Dutch-listed company, has been focusing on carpets, among other things, through its recyclable Niaga carpet brand. Normally carpets can't be recycled, as too many layers and materials are glued together, so unwanted carpets get buried or burned. DSM has calculated that if all the carpets wasted each year were laid in Central Park, it would be the tallest thing in New York City by 2040. Dutch company DyeCoo has developed a process of dyeing cloth without using water or additional chemicals, and its investors include Nike and IKEA.

Royal Ahrend, a Dutch office furniture company, produces furniture that is more long-lasting than so-called 'fast furniture' – up to 90 per cent of discarded office furniture in Europe ends up incinerated or in landfill, according to the European Federation of Furniture Manufacturers – and has also experimented with recrafting existing furniture, taking old upholstery from airline KLM to make material for tabletops.

Waste management also plays a role in the circular economy – particularly companies involved in recycling.

Some expressed caution about such companies during the pandemic, however. Analysts at HSBC warned in April 2020 that recycling was under pressure, with recycling collections falling amid the widespread lockdowns around the world: 'As economies struggle in coming months, we expect investments in recycling facilities and capacity may slow.' That could affect smaller businesses and those such as Biffa, a UK-based waste management company that HSBC had previously argued was a circular-economy success story. But the hit might only be short term. Another UK recycling company, Viridor, was snapped up by US private equity firm KKR in March 2020 for more than £4bn, in what was notably one of the first large transactions agreed during the market turmoil triggered by the pandemic. In a sign of confidence that such companies have a long life ahead of them, KKR told the *Financial Times* that Viridor was 'incredibly resilient, incredibly defensive and supported by long-term contracts with local authorities'.

French company Veolia has been partnering with some of the world's largest consumer companies to focus on packaging: in 2018, it announced a three-year partnership with Unilever to improve waste collection and recycling to help create a circular economy for plastics waste. It also worked with Procter & Gamble on their UK plant for manufacturing Gillette aerosols, working out what materials could be recycled or treated and eventually helping the plant reprocess every component of the spray cans. Both Veolia and Viridor are also involved in so-called waste-to-energy, whereby waste can be burned to produce energy, saving methane and other emissions that would have been produced had it been sent to landfill (though some air pollution is still created in this process).

One of the top holdings in the Impax Environmental Markets fund is DS Smith, a FTSE 100-listed packaging company in the UK that has been expanding in the US, developing environmentally friendly packaging solutions and using recycled paper and cardboard to make new packaging. Companies like this can also help address the issue of so-called scope 3 emissions, which take into account emissions indirectly caused by a company through their supply chain.

The sharing economy is also part of the circular-economy movement: the emphasis being on consumers owning fewer things and instead renting or sharing. Lift-sharing services like Uber or Lyft are one obvious example, while in China, start-up YCloset, which allows users to rent clothes and jewellery, attracted investment from Chinese technology giant Alibaba in 2018.

A circular economy in fashion could also be given a boost by the coronavirus pandemic, as people practising social distancing look to refresh their wardrobes cheaply or repair what they already own. In April 2020, analysts at HSBC said that they saw 'significant opportunities' for fashion companies that were exploring things like rental clothing platforms and repair services. Such companies include H&M, Patagonia and the RealReal. Not only would it give them a source of income in uncertain times; it would also make them prepared for possible future policies from the European Union, for example, which has been focusing on waste in the textile industry.

Zero emission pledges

Larger companies are also making efforts to embrace the circular economy. AB InBev, the drinks company that owns Budweiser and Corona beer, plans to ensure that 100 per cent of its products are in packaging that is either returnable or mostly recycled by 2025. It's also working with its suppliers on recycling rates, as part of the increased focus on scope 3 emissions. And outdoor clothing company Patagonia has introduced a repair system for its products, charging a fee to fix clothing that is falling apart or broken rather than requiring consumers to buy something new.

Other companies are embracing the idea of energy efficiency by making zero-carbon pledges, in much the same way as governments and cities across the world have promised to become carbon neutral by 2050 or earlier. That opens up an opportunity to invest in those that are 'best in class', as mentioned elsewhere in this book: companies in any industry that are doing more to address their own carbon footprint, as opposed to those whose main business is aimed at mitigating climate change.

'It's a problem that the climate narrative is associated with pure green [companies],' says Zoe Knight, head of HSBC's centre of sustainable finance. 'It should be about transition: we need to get towards products that are honest about financing transition, and that comes back to disclosure.'

A report by the CDP found that just 100 companies – all fossil fuel companies, perhaps unsurprisingly – had been the source of more than 70 per cent of global emissions between 1988 and 2015. As we saw in Chapter 4, professional investors have increasingly been putting pressure on the companies they invest in to reduce their carbon footprint. The CDP also produces an A List each year of the companies that are showing the best leadership on climate change issues – those that go beyond disclosing their emissions to actually taking positive action to reduce them. The list is long – 182 companies made the grade in 2019 – and includes many household names and companies that one would not normally associate with climate change mitigation due to the nature of their business, like Ford Motors, US banks BNY Mellon and Citigroup, Philip Morris and Nestlé.

Yet investing in Philip Morris, the tobacco company that produces Marlboro cigarettes among others, will probably not form part of many people's idea of investing to save the planet. It is another example of some of the contradictions we've seen in this book that investors can face when trying to decide what to invest in and what to avoid, and how their money can be put to best use.

This chapter was the final of our thematic forays into climate change investing. Now, in our conclusion, we'll look at how investors are trying to understand and measure climate risk across their investment portfolios.

What can you do?

- Low-risk investors: a lower-risk way of investing in companies that are energy efficient is to pick the largest, most liquid mainstream companies that have promised to drastically reduce their emissions or become carbon neutral. The CDP's A List is a good place to start, but environmental funds will also pick some of these companies in their holdings.
- Medium-risk investors: investing in companies that are supporting and enabling the transition to the circular economy and more energy-efficient practices is one way to play this theme. These can include companies involved in building insulation, software, waste management or semiconductors. Such companies are likely to be owned by environmental or climate change funds. So far it's been rare for funds to specifically give themselves an energy-efficiency label, perhaps because the idea has less direct appeal than other sectors.
- High-risk investors: again, venture capital or private equity funds do not tend to specialise in energy efficiency, but will address it through their cleantech or environmental offerings more

generally. New technologies such as those required for energy-efficient air conditioners, or start-up consumer apps offering clothes rental or clothes swaps, are some of the areas of innovation where early-stage companies are looking for cash from investors.

Conclusion:
What Does the Future Hold?

How hot is your portfolio? Is it 1.5 degrees, 2 degrees, or even 3 degrees? The question may sound a bit mad, but it could become increasingly normal, as the investment world and bank analysts wake up to the need to assess the risk of investing in the era of climate change. That's according to Mark Lewis, head of climate change investment research at BNP Paribas's asset management arm in Paris – and, in a sign that banks are looking to recruit experts on climate change, former head of research at think tank Carbon Tracker. He predicts that investors may be challenged in the future on how hot their portfolios are – meaning how their investments would fare in a world where temperatures rose at different levels. You can imagine that a 1.5 degrees portfolio would do well if it was stocked full of companies that had helped to bring down emissions, for example, whereas a 3 degrees portfolio might cope a bit better with owning fossil fuel companies. But the idea is that everyone should be aiming to hold as 'cool' a portfolio as possible. Japan's Government Pension Investment Fund, for example, which is one of the most climate-conscious pension funds in the world, has reportedly calculated that the temperature of its portfolio is

3.7 degrees, and is trying to manage this down to a lower temperature.

Lewis points out that there's been a rush at investment banks to cover the climate change sector – an area that historically was under-researched. Fund managers rely on research from analysts at big investment banks, from Goldman Sachs and Morgan Stanley to Lewis's own bank in France, BNP Paribas, to research companies and give their opinion on whether shares are too pricey or looking cheap: whether something is a buy, a sell or a hold. Of course there is a lot of opportunism in the banking world: as ESG and particularly climate change has become trendy, analysts have started churning out research on the topic. Less cynically, you could say this is investment banks responding to demand: Lewis says that pension funds and fund managers were ahead of the curve when it came to expressing an interest in measuring the impact of climate change on their investments, and analysts are now scrabbling to keep up. But this need to devise some sort of way of measuring and predicting the climate risk that companies are exposed to is unlikely to go away.

In fact, analysts now believe that any investor who is not investing with climate change in mind could be exposing themselves to serious risk. The divide between sustainable and 'normal' investment will not hold for much longer. The UN's Principles for Responsible Investment (PRI) body warns that financial markets haven't really worked out how to price climate transition risk. It warns that not only will such policy change accelerate – with the bulk of it predicted to come in 2023–5 – but it will be sudden and forceful as governments realise they should have acted sooner, meaning that the effects on various industries will be worse. Financial markets around the world haven't priced in a forceful policy response to climate change in the near term. What if subsidies for oil and gas suddenly end, for example? Or cars with internal combustion engines are banned altogether? The PRI says that this forceful policy response is 'a highly likely outcome, leaving portfolios exposed to significant risk'.

Working out climate change risk is a headache for individual investors too. Liesel Pritzker Simmons, whose fortune is so large she has her own family office, recalls attending a meeting of an investment committee she was on and watching the financial adviser give a presentation on the market. It included a slide pointing out that climate change posed a financial risk. 'I said, OK, what is the climate risk analysis of this portfolio? Crickets,' she says, referring to the blank silence she was met with. She thinks there is a huge market opportunity for advisers to try to work this risk out properly. 'At this point, even for a client like me where I have the interest and the resources to do a full climate risk analysis of my portfolio, it's not easy: it's not a phone call away; it's a year's worth of work.'

Analysts at Barclays[*] also think this lack of rigorous

---

* Barclays research report: Fundamental ESG themes for 2020, 2 April 2020.

risk analysis is an opportunity, arguing that there is a role for consultants to help companies calculate their ESG risk and verify reported figures on emissions. That will ultimately benefit investors both large and small. 'It may be that companies are more likely to get away with dishonest reporting of sustainability issues than they would with dishonest financial reporting due to the lack of regulatory oversight and complexities with calculating data such as carbon emissions,' they write. 'In the longer term, this should change as investors step up their due diligence and engagement around ESG issues.'

Some of the policies the PRI predicts are things we've discussed in this book, as they are already creating conditions for climate change-friendly companies to thrive. These include a phase-out of coal, bans on internal combustion engine (ICE) vehicles, carbon pricing and energy efficiency. On the first two in particular, the PRI has set dates in mind: it predicts an early coal phase-out for first-mover countries by 2030, then the steady retirement of coal-fired power generation after 2030 in lagging countries. It predicts an ICE sales ban for first-mover countries by 2035, with other countries following suit as the automotive industry reaches a tipping point.

Some authorities are, as we've seen, already introducing such measures. Cities are often leading the charge. Paris, Madrid, Amsterdam and Athens have announced bans on diesel and ICE vehicles by 2025 and 2030. The UK – one of the few countries to set a zero emissions target by 2050 – in 2020 brought forward a ban on selling new petrol, diesel or hybrid cars from 2040 to 2035.

Most EU countries have coal phase-out plans, as do the UK and Canada.

It is clear that governments and regulation play a huge role in incentivising companies and consumers to reduce their carbon footprint. Some people argue that there is little point in consumers making efforts to recycle, or reduce their personal emissions, when governments are not taking enough steps to enforce the rules, or when consumers in other countries aren't doing as much. But if regulations do come into effect, as the PRI predicts, it will have made good financial sense to position investment portfolios accordingly. And green innovation, it notes, will provide first-mover competitive advantages and reduce transition costs.

In January 2020, index provider MSCI said that *all* investors – not just sustainable investors – should incorporate ESG principles in their investments to mitigate the risks of climate change. Its chief executive, Henry Fernandez, warned: 'The world is rapidly evolving due to dramatic environmental, social and governance shifts, including the effects and implications of climate change and the move to a low-carbon economy, which will significantly impact the pricing of financial assets and the risk and return of investments, and lead to a large-scale reallocation of capital over the next few decades.' MSCI's head of ESG, meanwhile, Remy Pascal, predicts a 'revolution' whereby within a few years it will become the norm to hold an ESG fund, rather than the struggle it can be now to convince your pension or financial adviser to offer you one.

This comes back to the debate earlier in this book on divestment, and the concerns of some pension fund trustees, for example, that by avoiding certain stocks they are narrowing their investment universe in a way that might hurt the end investors. But on both MSCI and the PRI's reckoning, it could be that *not* avoiding companies at particular risk of policy changes could hurt the end investors more.

The real risks

In order for investors to say how hot their portfolios are, they need to be able to measure the climate change risk of their investments in some sort of agreed way. That is not currently possible. But governments and regulators are working on it. One issue is that most companies currently only disclose, if they disclose anything at all, their so-called scope 1 and scope 2 emissions, but not their scope 3 emissions. Scope 1 emissions are direct emissions from things that companies own. Scope 2 covers indirect emissions from the electricity or other power used by the company. Scope 3 covers other indirect emissions in a company's supply chain and also, in the case of an oil and gas company, for example, the emissions caused by consumers when they use the energy. If you think about this in the home, for example, your scope 1 emissions would come from boiling water (on a gas hob) to make a cup of tea. Your scope 2 emissions come from putting the dishwasher on afterwards to wash up the cup. And your scope 3 emissions come from the companies that produced both the kettle and the dishwasher and transported them to your home.

Because scope 3 emissions are basically created by other companies, they can be quite hard to measure. But they usually account for the vast majority of a company's total emissions – the Carbon Trust has estimated as much as 90 per cent in some cases. So it's important for companies to take account of them, so that they can identify hotspots in their emissions supply chain and make conscious decisions either to encourage suppliers to reduce their carbon footprint or switch suppliers.

In the absence of internationally agreed standards to measure scope 3 emissions, any implied temperature of a portfolio, notes Mark Lewis, will be 'wildly inaccurate' if these are not taken into account. However, measures are afoot to improve matters. In March 2020, the European Union published guidelines for a new taxonomy of sustainable finance, which include requirements for all companies to disclose scope 3 emissions by 2024.

There is starting to be some acknowledgement of scope 3 emissions even among the oil and gas companies. In 2020, BP and Shell both announced net zero emissions goals for 2050 that they said would also take account of scope 3 emissions (if not fully target them, with some environmentalists still critical of the lack of detail).

Some professional investors are part of an initiative called PCAF – the Partnership for Carbon Accounting Financials – which enables financial institutions to assess and disclose greenhouse gas emissions of loans and investments. Triodos, one of the founding members of PCAF, says that encouraging companies to work out their scope 3 emissions is one of the key remits of the group.

A price for carbon

One of the main policies that investors, regulators, companies and even fossil fuel executives argue will be most effective in combating climate change is carbon pricing: a tax on the most polluting fossil fuels. Such a tax would encourage oil and gas companies to switch to lower polluting sources and invest more in renewables. It could also raise revenues for governments that could be used to offset the harmful macroeconomic effects – reduced employment and investment – of higher energy prices, according to a very readable December 2019 article for the IMF journal *Finance & Development*, which calculates that a $35 per tonne tax on carbon dioxide emissions in 2030, for example, would typically increase prices for coal, electricity and gasoline by about 100, 25 and 10 per cent respectively. A $35 tax would not be enough to keep emissions below 2 per cent, though – for that, the IMF paper says that a global average of $75 a tonne would be needed.

Carbon pricing is politically a loaded topic. It is likely to require global cooperation, as first-movers could suffer from a competition advantage from other nations if it's not universally adopted. Yet attempts to agree on a global market for carbon pricing at the last annual UN climate change convention, COP25, in Madrid in December 2019 flopped. The US government under Trump has been particularly resistant to global cooperation on climate change and carbon pricing, having told the UN in November 2019 that it would withdraw from the Paris Agreement the following year. Analysts at UBS have predicted that, due to the difficulties in introducing global green regulations, a more likely scenario is that individual governments will restrict fossil fuel investment, leading to political success that other countries would want to emulate.

Yet carbon pricing is by no means off the table. The US secretary of agriculture became the first member of the Trump cabinet to endorse the idea in February 2020, despite resistance from farmers who argued that it would harm their industry. And the idea was starting to gain traction with Wall Street, too. J. P. Morgan boss Jamie Dimon – who has come under pressure from environmentalists concerned about his bank's financing of oil and gas companies – told the *Financial Times* it would 'generate significant emission reductions, promote innovation and protect Americans from rising costs'.

The Climate Leadership Council, a US-focused policy institute founded in 2017 to promote the idea of a carbon tax, set out a roadmap for such a tax in February 2020, arguing that if followed, it could cut US emissions in half by 2035. Some of the world's largest polluters, including BP and ExxonMobil, are part of the council, along with J. P. Morgan and Goldman Sachs. The carbon pricing discussions were set to be revived at the 26th UN climate summit, COP26, which was due to be held in Glasgow in 2020 and was delayed to the following year thanks to the pandemic.

An analysis by the consultancy Oliver Wyman conducted before the pandemic-related oil price crash warned that oil and gas companies would be two to three times more likely to default on their debt if even only a $50 a tonne carbon tax were introduced. The report, published in February 2020, said that at that time, not one single bank had devised a satisfactory strategy of measuring climate change risk in corporate debt.

Many professional investors believe that more regulation via a carbon tax will start to make it easier to assess the climate risk of portfolios. 'Far too few people in the investment industry have focused on really trying to understand the question of what impact carbon prices have on the value of different investments,' says Andy Howard, global head of sustainable investment at Schroders. 'The next 10 years are incredibly important as this is when we need to turn the corner – so the likelihood of regulatory intervention is quite high and the biggest stick that regulators wield is carbon pricing.' For now, Schroders has built its own model of how to assess the climate risk of companies, including modelling how it would fare under a carbon tax, the impact of new technologies and the cost of stranded assets. 'For a lot of people, climate change is a way of selling funds rather than an investment risk. For us, it is an unavoidable and potentially very disruptive risk we have to understand. It isn't a marketing strapline.'

Climate change may also require financial markets to change the way they think about risk. 'Our friends in the financial industry are lazy,' says Jeremy Oppenheim of Systemiq. 'The way risk analysis is typically done is that it's backward-looking, based on historic data, and it tends to assume the probability distribution of events is stationary.' If something happens that is normally a 1-in-100-year event, he explains, financial risk analysts will still assign it that low-risk level in the future too. 'The problem that climate change poses is it asks you to take all those three points and turn them on their head.'

Global standards

While carbon pricing will be one global standard, there is also a need for more coordinated regulation on what sustainability means. We have seen that a lack of consistency on the definition of ESG, for example, when creating funds can confuse consumers.

Accountants too have a role to play. Writing in the *Financial Times*, Gillian Tett has warned of the 'alphabet soup of standards' when it comes to measuring companies' exposure to climate risk. There is the Amsterdam-based Global Reporting Initiative, or there is the San Francisco-based Sustainability Accounting Standards Board. There is Mark Carney's Taskforce for Climate-Related Financial Disclosure system for banks and there is MSCI's ESG indices. But at Davos in 2020, the big four accounting firms, Deloitte, PwC, KPMG and EY, met with chief executives and investors to discuss coordinating standards for risk that all investors could follow.

At the end of 2019, the European Union agreed a historic deal on how to classify green investments, marking the first time a global regulator had designed a labelling system for what is or isn't a sustainable financial product. The move was partly aimed at combating greenwashing, with plans to put an 'eco-label' on retail financial products to help consumers make informed decisions. But it was also aimed at helping institutional investors to finance green technology, channelling a wave of money into carbon-neutral projects.

Regulators are already putting greenwashing risks high up on their radars. In January 2020, Italian oil major ENI was slapped on the wrist by the country's regulator with a €5m fine. The company had been marketing a particular brand of diesel as 'green'. Yet the diesel was made with palm oil, which has a troubled environmental record. In making its ruling, the watchdog said it had been 'particularly deceitful' to use the term 'green diesel' given the emissions associated with palm oil, which require precious forests to be cleared to make way for the crop.

A fine of just €5m is not much for an oil giant. But it was hailed as significant by Italian consumer groups. The president of Italian consumer association Movimento Difesa del Cittadino, which was one of the groups to file the complaint, told the *Wall Street Journal* that it was 'the first important sanction for "greenwashing" over misleading advertising messages about how green a product really is'.

It was also viewed as an indicator of what is likely to come. We've seen examples in this book of big companies getting in trouble for making false advertising claims to consumers about how green their products are. But it is rapidly becoming a headache for the financial industry as well, as consumer interest in climate change investment products grows and banks and investment firms fall over themselves trying to provide them.

Fines from national regulators over greenwashing are still in their infancy. Yet they are expected to rise. Noting the significant increase in green financial products, the UK's financial regulator, the Financial Conduct Authority, said in October 2019 that it would challenge firms where it saw potential greenwashing and take action to prevent consumers being misled. 'It is not always clear what firms or consumers mean by, or expect from, "green products",' it noted, adding that sometimes it is hard to tell the difference between supposedly sustainable funds and normal investment products. 'On the face of it, some of these do not appear to have materially different exposures to products that do not have such a label.' In the absence of common standards, 'there is a risk that consumers suffer harm from "greenwashing"'.

Catherine Howarth, the chief executive of UK responsible investment group ShareAction, told the *Financial Times* in 2019: 'Quite a bit of greenwashing is going on out there . . . We don't want responsible investment to be the next mis-selling scandal.' The European Securities and Markets Authority said in February 2020 that it was looking for evidence of greenwashing, with its chairperson arguing that 'we need to be careful to ensure that investors do not end up buying products which are marketed as sustainable when in reality they are not'.

Some central banks are going to start including climate change risks in their stress tests of how well companies will fare in certain scenarios. Mark Carney said in December 2019 that the Bank of England would start asking companies to model their exposures to the Paris Agreement's targets.

Carney – the former head of the Bank of England and now UN Special Envoy for Climate Action and Finance – has been one of the most vocal and prominent financiers on the need for financial markets to measure climate risk properly. In 2015, he gave a speech at Lloyd's of London that is now famous in sustainable investment circles for introducing the concept of 'the tragedy of the horizon' – a play on the tragedy of the commons theory, whereby individuals spoil shared resources for everyone by only acting in their own interests. Under the tragedy of the horizon, Carney said, the impacts of climate change will be largely felt by future generations, so it is hard to incentivise the current generation to act. Normally the horizon for central bankers to consider financial stability, he said, is 10 years into the future – by which point it would be too late to act. Changing this mindset would be a further example of the systemic change that Jeremy Oppenheim at Systemiq believes is necessary.

Carney also highlighted the risks to insurers, which had already been increasing thanks to adverse weather effects. Investors worry that companies deemed to be more at risk from climate change will find it harder to get insurance or loans from banks in future, making them riskier investments in other ways too. US oil and gas company Devon Energy Corp said in February 2020 that banks' concerns over climate change could 'make it more difficult to fund our operations'.

But Carney also said that the huge shifts in mindset that climate change will require are opportunities for the financial industry. 'Financing the de-carbonisation of our economy is a major opportunity for insurers as long-term investors,' he said, adding: '"Green" finance cannot conceivably remain a niche interest over the medium term.'

In short, a lot of different groups in the financial world need to coordinate and do more to help people invest to save the planet. But investors already have plenty of options. Armed with the information in this book, you can now ask yourself: do you want to ditch the world's most polluting companies from your portfolio? Or do you want to reward those making efforts to cut their emissions, to invest in renewables and to help the world during its energy transition? Are you one of the wealthy individuals who want to back the next big thing in climate change tech, be it lab-grown meat, electric aircraft or energy-efficient air conditioners? Or are you simply keen to make sure you've considered the effect of climate change on your investments over the long term, if you're saving for a pension or hoping to pass money on to dependants? As we've seen, there's no right or wrong answer to any of these questions.

It's also worth noting that due to our focus on positive solutions, one area we haven't looked at in detail in this book is an adaptation strategy. Some investors are hedging their bets and buying companies that are likely to do well if global warming gets bad. Such bets might include backup power generator companies, for example, where demand will be higher as more extreme weather events such as hurricanes cause power cuts. Impax Asset Management is an investor in Generac, for example, a US backup power specialist that sees storms as a big driver of its market.

In general, professional investors agree that in addition to better regulation to protect consumers, and awareness of the way in which sustainable or ESG terms are used, the financial industry also needs to widen access for retail investors looking to help the environment with their money. While equities have been an obvious first port of call, and green bonds have become more popular, some investors are now turning to other areas as well. UBS, for example, has looked at how high-yield debt – bonds issued by companies that need to pay investors a higher yield because higher risks are involved in lending to them – could have a role in sustainable investors' portfolios if investors engage with the companies to improve their governance, for example, with the additional benefit of having an asset class that pays higher returns.

The whole world can't dump oil stocks tomorrow – and it would probably be unwise even if it could, as oil and gas companies have deep pockets for research and development into new renewable technologies. But gradually the sands are shifting, and investors are getting more and more options.

Beyond the pandemic

The arrival of the coronavirus at the start of 2020 was of course completely unexpected by investors of all stripes. Stock markets crashed as governments shut their economies down. Having hit a record high in mid February, the S&P 500 – the main benchmark for the US stock market – plunged 34 per cent in little over four weeks. In mid March, it had its worst one-day fall since the crash of October 1987, losing 12 per cent.

This could have been a huge test for climate change investing: was it just a fad, which would disappear as investors hunted returns from any source to make up for their lost income?

The early signs were that it was *not* just a fad. To start with, ESG funds outperformed the initial stock market crashes (meaning in this instance that they lost less than other funds). While the S&P 500 lost more than 13 per cent from the start of 2020 to 9 April, some of the biggest ESG investment funds outperformed that over the same time period, an analysis by S&P Global showed. The Brown Advisory Sustainable Growth Fund, for example, lost just 5.4 per cent. It will not have hurt that its two biggest holdings were Microsoft and Amazon, two tech companies that benefited from the lockdown through online conferencing and home deliveries. The chief executive of Calvert, an investment manager that also had an outperforming ESG fund, told S&P Global: 'It's clear that companies that had been thoughtful about managing other environmental or social risks were ready for any kind of situation and have reacted quite well.'

The G in ESG funds probably did some heavy lifting during this period. Companies with good governance are likely to have strong balance sheets and stable dividends, so a better bet during a recession than, say, cyclical companies like airlines. Rachel Whittaker, a sustainable investing strategist at UBS, says that, in general, sustainability can be seen as a proxy for good management: 'ESG companies are likely to be higher-quality companies, better capitalised and have stronger balance sheets and weather the downturn better.'

But the E was also relevant too. ESG funds almost certainly hold fewer oil and gas companies and airlines than normal funds, and both these types of companies were hammered during the coronavirus lockdown as the oil price plummeted and airlines were grounded due to lack of demand. Hortense Bioy at Morningstar said there had also not been huge outflows of investors from ESG funds over the first few months of the downturn.

'I think it's testament to the stickiness of ESG investments that we didn't see outflows compared to the main market. Investors in these strategies really think long and hard about that approach and are driven by their values – when markets fall they panic less than other investors.'

The relative strength of ESG fund performance can be seen as backing the argument that investing sustainably does not necessarily mean giving up returns. Yet in general, drawing investment conclusions based on short-term performance data is not advisable. Sustainable investors – indeed, any investors – generally say that it is more important to focus on the longer-term case for holding companies that are adapting to climate change, rather than focusing on short-term shocks. Global stock markets were incredibly volatile during the initial lockdown period in any case, with a huge rebound in April that saw some markets claw back all their losses for the year.

Some predicted that the silver lining of the pandemic, if there was one, was that it was improving the environment, as coal factories shut down and blue skies were observed over normally polluted cities. But while there was a drop in carbon emissions, it only went so far. The climate science website Carbon Brief estimated that emissions in 2020 would be 5 to 6 per cent lower than the previous year – the largest fall on record, but not enough. Even if that rate continued for the rest of the decade, it would still not cut emissions sufficiently to restrict global temperature rises to 1.5 degrees. A UN

Environment Programme (UNEP) report in 2019 said that global greenhouse gas emissions needed to fall by 7.6 per cent each year between 2020 and 2030 in order to stick to the 1.5 degrees target.

Fortunately, there was evidence that the longer-term case for being mindful of climate change was not being ignored as the coronavirus lockdowns spread across the world. Companies and investors made the right noises. The new chief executive of BP, Bernard Looney, said in April that even though BP's share price had hit a 24-year low in March, it was not going to renege on a zero emissions pledge it had made in February. Noting the effect people were having on oil demand by flying less and working at home, he told the *Financial Times*: 'I don't see the climate debate going away . . . [It] may be enhanced by what we're seeing.'

We've also seen that in March, BlackRock doubled down on its promise to hold more companies to account over climate change, repeating its call for companies to report climate risk in line with the Taskforce for Climate-Related Financial Disclosures guidelines, and warning that it could vote against directors if those disclosures were inadequate.

There was a general feeling that the pandemic didn't alter the longer-term risks and opportunities that climate change was going to create for investors. The UN PRI said in March that investors should ensure that responsible ESG approaches remained at the forefront of investor activities despite the coronavirus crisis, and that the future economic recovery should consider how the financial system should function to ensure sustainable outcomes.

Some went further and saw the pandemic as an opportunity. In the first few weeks of the crisis, companies that were firing workers rather than furloughing them or engaging in other unethical business practices were roundly criticised in the press and on social media. Some predicted that it was now the time for the S in ESG to shine. Analysts at Morgan Stanley said in March: 'With the disruption caused by the Covid-19 crisis, "social" considerations are back at the forefront of ESG. Corporate decisions affecting workers . . . have become increasingly important as a wider array of investors have begun looking at companies through an ESG lens.'

Analysts at Barclays predicted that the coronavirus crisis could even accelerate investors' interest in climate change, arguing that while ESG implementation might be delayed in the short term, 'it is unlikely to be abandoned in the long run – and it may even accelerate in a post-Covid-19 world'.

Of course, not all the developments were positive. The *Financial Times* warned in April that the coronavirus outbreak had delayed most of the big climate events and policy announcements expected in 2020. Glen Peters, research director at the Center for International Climate Research in Oslo, warned that climate might not be mentioned in policy discussions in the near term, telling the *Financial Times*: 'It's going to put a pause on anything climate related.' The UN's 26th summit on climate change, scheduled for November 2020 in Glasgow, was postponed until the following year. Rather symbolically, the conference centre that was supposed to stage the talks was converted into a hospital for coronavirus patients. The politics of climate change also came to the fore. Those who argue that steps to mitigate climate change aren't fair if they harm economic growth, particularly in emerging market economies where citizens have long wanted the freedom and wealth of a Western lifestyle, will find it particularly easy to argue that the economy should trump environmental concerns during a pandemic.

But attention also turned to how governments could use stimulus packages to 'Build Back Better' – by putting sustainability and climate change at the heart of plans to revive their economies. The United Nations used Earth Day on 22 April to call on governments to do precisely this, arguing that the huge amounts of money spent on recovering from the coronavirus should deliver new jobs and businesses through a clean, green transition. In addition, the UN said, where taxpayers' money had been used to save companies from going bust, it should be tied to achieving green jobs and sustainable growth. Public funds should flow to sustainable sectors and projects that help the environment and the climate, while fossil fuel subsidies should end. 'We need to turn the recovery into a real opportunity to do things right for the future,' the UN secretary general António Guterres said. Richard Curtis also used the 'Build Back Better' slogan when he announced his new Make My Money Matter campaign.

A report by McKinsey asked: 'Can the world afford to pay attention to climate change and the broader sustainability agenda at this time? Our firm belief is that we simply cannot afford to do otherwise.' The authors argued that it was not just that climate action would remain critical. They also made the point that investments in climate-resilient infrastructure and the transition to a lower-carbon future could help create much-needed jobs in an economic downturn.

'It may well be that this is going to be the beginning of a new era in many respects,' said Al Gore when I interviewed him for this book, reflecting on the future of sustainable investment while the world was in lockdown. 'I believe very strongly that the issue of the sustainability crisis and its largest manifestation, the climate crisis, are more important than ever to the investing world and this would not be the first time that a period of discontinuity served to accelerate changes that were building up before the discontinuity began.'

We may well be, as Gore puts it, on the cusp of a new era. Arguably the coronavirus pandemic has created even more will to combat climate change. The need for government support for various industries has created new opportunities for policy change, by linking bailouts to environmental promises. Environmental campaigners as well as some politicians have argued that airlines, for example, should not get a blank cheque but should make firm promises to cut emissions in return for funds. The head of the International Energy Agency, Fatih Birol, said that governments should put clean energy at the heart of stimulus plans, and use the current situation to step up their climate ambitions. Canada announced it would create 10,000 jobs in the energy sector through programmes to clean up disused oil wells and launch an emission reduction fund. Prime minister Justin Trudeau said: 'Just because we're in a health crisis doesn't mean we can neglect the environmental crisis.' After being ravaged by the coronavirus with one of the worst death tolls in Europe, Spain announced a draft law to cut emissions to net zero by 2050 as part of a pandemic recovery package.

In May, various investor groups including the IIGCC, the PRI and the CDP published a letter to governments around the world urging them to prioritise sustainability and mitigating climate change in their recovery plans, pointing out that this could create new jobs and make economies more resilient in the future. 'The path we choose in the coming months will have significant ramifications for our global economy and generations to come,' they wrote. 'Our organisations that work with investors stand ready to help governments to invest in a better, more resilient future.'

A study by Oxford University found that green economy recovery packages after the coronavirus – such as those encouraging energy efficiency, building charging networks for electric vehicles or planting trees – were likely to create more jobs and would actually be a better return on investments for governments, leading to longer-term savings. 'Tackling climate change is the answer to our economic problems,' lead author Cameron Hepburn told the *Guardian*.

As the lockdowns swept across the world, Israeli historian Yuval Noah Harari wrote a moving piece in the *Financial Times* about how humanity should react to the huge changes taking place, declaring that cooperation between nations was crucial at such times of upheaval: 'If we choose global solidarity, it will be a victory not only against the coronavirus, but against all future epidemics and crises that might assail humankind in the twenty-first century.'

If the investors we've studied in this book are right, this global solidarity could see governments, regulators and the financial industry working together to create a more sustainable economy that is fit for the future, an economy that all investors, big and small, can feel they helped to build.

Acknowledgements

Many people have helped me to write this book in many different ways. I would like to thank my agent, Laura West, for her support and positivity and my editors at Penguin, Martina O'Sullivan and Celia Buzuk, for their great and thoughtful edits, and to Jane Selley and Natalie Wall for their reassuring attention to all the details.

Lots of people kindly gave up their time to help me with the research for this book. Everyone I interviewed spoke freely and enthusiastically about their work either thinking up solutions to climate change problems, investing in them themselves or encouraging others to invest in them – all of which was very inspiring.

Others offered support in different ways. I would like to thank Roula Khalaf and James Lamont at the *Financial Times* in particular for allowing me to take the time to work on a personal project at a time when I was working on an important project at the newspaper as well. I'd like to thank other amazing colleagues at the *FT* who read sections of the book for me and offered their advice and support: thank you especially to Nathalie Thomas, Emiko Terazono, Tanya Powley and Billy Nauman.

A huge thank you also to the people in my life who told me I could get this done, even during a pandemic, and who offered motivational as well as emotional support: Naomi Wright, Rachel James, Bronwen Wilson Rashad, Amaleena Damlé, David Shariatmadari, Julia Tuffs, Becca Langton and many others.

And of course, thank you to my parents Finlay and Kathryn, and to Nik, for everything.

Index